Data Rookies Labs: Intro to Analytics with R

Hands On Practice for Beginners

Data Analytics Curriculum, LLC

About the Publisher

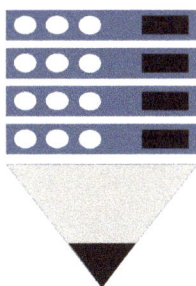

Data Analytics Curriculum

Data Analytics Curriculum, LLC creates approachable, visually engaging educational materials that make data science and technology accessible for learners from high school to college and independent study.

Please see our website or TPT online store for additional titles and resources such as slides, additional book forms, content (non lab) textbooks to accompany these labs, solution guides and other resources to help you teach and learn.

Additional resources available:

Website: https://www.dataanalyticscurriculum.com

Contents

Contents

Lab 1

Intro to R and RStudio

What is R and Why Use It?

R is a powerful and free programming language created specifically for statistical computing and data analysis. It has become popular across various fields such as data analytics, machine learning, and statistical analysis due to its extensive range of specialized packages tailored for data manipulation and interpretation. One of R's key strengths lies in its excellent data visualization capabilities, which allow users to create clear and insightful graphics. Additionally, it boasts strong libraries that support both statistical methods and machine learning techniques, making it a versatile tool for data professionals.

The language also benefits from a large and active community that contributes to its continuous improvement and offers support to users. Complementing R is RStudio, an Integrated Development Environment (IDE) that enhances the user experience by providing a more accessible interface, features like syntax highlighting, and various tools that help streamline the management of data projects, making it easier for both beginners and experienced users to work efficiently with R.

Part 1: Installing R and RStudio

Step 1: Download and Install R

Visit the R Project website: Go to https://www.r-project.org/

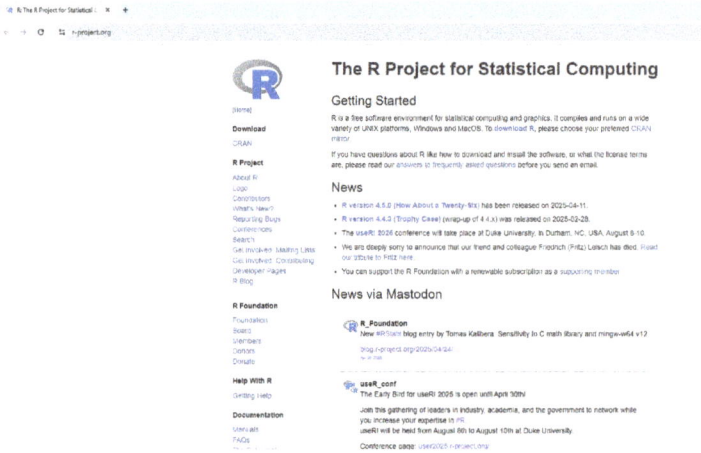

To install R, start by clicking on "CRAN" (Comprehensive R Archive Network) in the left sidebar of the website. Next, choose a mirror location that is close to you—any mirror in the USA works well for users in the United States. Then, select your operating system. For Windows, click on "Download R for Windows," then "base," and finally "Download R 4.x.x for Windows." Mac users should click on "Download R for macOS" and download the appropriate .pkg file for their system. If you are using Linux, follow the specific instructions provided for your distribution. Once the download is complete, run the installer and proceed with the default settings by clicking "Next" through the installation prompts.

Step 2: Download and Install RStudio

Note: You must install R first before installing RStudio, as RStudio requires R to function.

Visit RStudio's website: Go to https://posit.co/downloads/

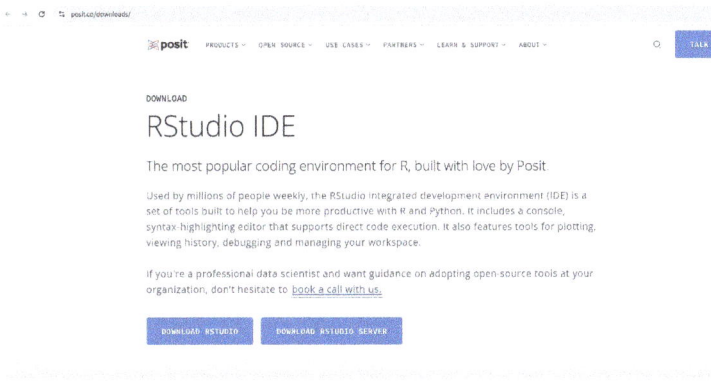

To install RStudio, scroll down the webpage until you find the section for RStudio Desktop, which is the free version. Click on "Download RStudio Desktop," then choose and download the installer that matches your operating system. Once the download is complete, run the installer and proceed with the default settings by simply clicking "Next" through the setup process.

Step 3: Verify Installation

Open RStudio (not R directly - we'll always use RStudio)

You should see a window with four panes (or three if it's your first time). In the bottom-left pane (Console), you should see something like:

If you see this, congratulations! You're ready to start using R.

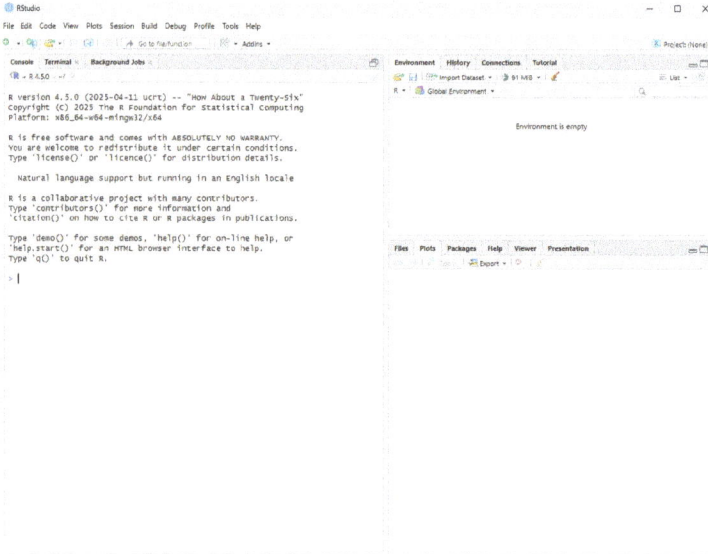

Part 2: The RStudio Interface

When you open RStudio, you'll see several panes. Initially there are three however go under file and do new R Script and the Script Editor appears.

Script Editor (Top-Left)

The Script Editor, located in the top-left panel of RStudio, is where you write and save your R scripts. It functions like a text editor specifically designed for writing R code, allowing you to organize and save your work for future use. From this panel, you can easily run individual lines or entire sections of code directly to the Console, making it a convenient space for developing and testing your code as you work through data analysis tasks.

Console (Bottom-Left)

The Console, found in the bottom-left panel of RStudio, is where R commands are executed. You can type commands directly into this space and see the results appear immediately below, making it useful for quick tests or interactive work. It's also where any code you run from the Script Editor will be processed, allowing you to view outputs, error messages, and other feedback in real time.

Environment/History (Top-Right)

The Environment/History panel, located in the top-right corner of RStudio, provides useful information about your current R session. The Environment tab displays all the data objects you've created, such as datasets, variables, and functions, allowing you to keep track of what's available in your workspace. The History tab keeps a record of all the commands you've run, making it easy to review, reuse, or modify previous code without having to retype it from memory.

Files/Plots/Packages/Help (Bottom-Right)

The Files/Plots/Packages/Help panel, located in the bottom-right corner of RStudio, serves several important functions. The Files tab lets you browse the files and folders on your computer, making it easy to locate and open your work. The Plots tab displays any graphs or visualizations you generate in R, allowing you to review and navigate through them. The Packages tab is where you can manage your R packages—these are add-on tools that extend R's capabilities, and you can install, load, or update them from this tab. Finally, the Help tab provides access to R's built-in documentation, offering detailed explanations and usage examples for functions and packages whenever you need guidance.

Part 3: Basic R Concepts

As a data analytics student, you'll primarily be running existing scripts rather than writing code from scratch. THIS IS NOT A PROGRAMMING COURSE OR BOOK. It is nice to have a programming background however the focus here is on USING and modifying existing scripts to perform data analytics tasks. You should be able to do this with a minimal programming background and should need to do little programming from scratch.

Working with Scripts

To open an existing R script in RStudio, go to the File menu, click on "Open File," and then select your .R file from your computer. Once your script is open, you can run your code in several ways. To execute a single line, place your cursor on that line and press Ctrl+Enter on Windows or Cmd+Enter on Mac. If you want to run multiple lines at once, highlight the lines you want to run and use the same keyboard shortcut. To run the entire script all at once, press Ctrl+Shift+Enter on Windows or Cmd+Shift+Enter on Mac. These shortcuts make it easy to test and execute your code efficiently.

Watch the output of running the script in the Console.

Understanding R Objects

In R, an object is simply a named piece of data that you create and store in your workspace. If you're new to programming, think of an object as a container that holds something—like a number, a list of names, a dataset, or even a graph. When you run code in R, you're often creating or modifying these objects. For example, if you type x <- 5, you're creating an object named x that stores the number 5. R has different types of objects depending on what kind of data you're working with. These include vectors (lists of values), data frames (tables of data), matrices (grids of numbers), and

6

more. Understanding objects is important because everything you do in R—whether analyzing data, creating plots, or running models—usually involves creating and using these objects.

When you run scripts, you'll create different types of data objects. Primarily we will be creating or reading data frame objects either by typing in data or uploading a csv file for use in this book.

R Code

```
# Numbers

my_number <- 5

# Text (character strings)

my_text <- "Hello Data Mining"

# Vectors (lists of values)

my_numbers <- c(1, 2, 3, 4, 5)

my_names <- c("Alice", "Bob", "Charlie")

# Data frames (like Excel spreadsheets)

my_data <- data.frame(

name = c("Alice", "Bob", "Charlie"),

age = c(25, 30, 35),

score = c(85, 92, 78)
```

```
)
```

Reading Data Files

Most data analytics work starts with loading data in a preexisting file. These files can be read into R – the most easy way is to use csv files as these have no meta data or formatting (they are clean). Other files such as Excel require special packages to be loaded (see below on definition of a package). After data is loaded several functions allow you to view the data easily to validate the upload before using the data in analytics.

```
R Code
# Reading CSV files

data <- read.csv("mydata.csv")

# Reading Excel files (requires readxl package)

library(readxl)

data <- read_excel("mydata.xlsx")

# Viewing your data

View(data) # Opens data in a new tab

head(data) # Shows first 6 rows

summary(data) # Shows basic statistics
```

Part 4: R Packages

R packages are collections of functions, data, and documentation that extend the basic functionality of R, making it easier to perform specialized types of analysis. You can think of them as add-on toolkits designed for specific tasks, such as data visualization, machine learning, time series analysis, or text mining. Most R packages are open source and are created and shared by members of the global R community, including researchers, developers, and data professionals. These packages are typically hosted on CRAN (the Comprehensive R Archive Network), which is the official repository, but others may also be found on platforms like GitHub. Installing a package is simple: you can use the install.packages("package_name") command in the Console, or you can go to the Packages tab in RStudio and use the interface to search for and install packages. Once installed, packages need to be loaded into your session using the library(package_name) function before you can use their tools.

Installing Packages

You only need to install a package once (downloading it form online source) and then it will live on your local machine (unless you delete the files where it is stored or otherwise alter things).

```
R Code
# Install a single packageinstall.packages("ggplot2")


# Install multiple packagesinstall.packages(c("dplyr", "tidyr",
"caret"))
```

9

Loading Packages

You need to load packages every time you start RStudio so that they are available in the current working project environment.

```
R Code
# Load a packagelibrary(ggplot2)

# Or multiple packages

library(dplyr)

library(tidyr)

library(caret)
```

Essential Packages for data analytics

Here are some packages often used in data analytics (some of which we will use in labs in coming chapters).

- **dplyr**: Data manipulation (filtering, sorting, summarizing)

- **ggplot2**: Creating beautiful visualizations

- **caret**: Machine learning and classification

- **randomForest**: Random forest algorithms

- **e1071**: Support vector machines and other ML algorithms

- **cluster**: Clustering analysis

- **arules**: Association rule mining

• **rpart**: Decision trees

Part 5: Common Script Patterns

When working with R scripts, you typically start by loading your dataset—for example, from a CSV file—and then perform a quick exploration to understand its size, column names, structure, and summary statistics. In R, many operations you perform are done using functions, which are like little machines or tools that take some input, process it, and give you an output. For example, read.csv() is a function that reads data from a CSV file and loads it into R. Functions always have a name followed by parentheses, where you put any information they need, called arguments. Here's how you might load data and explore it:

```
# Load data

data <- read.csv("sales_data.csv")

# Quick exploration

dim(data) # Dimensions (rows, columns)

names(data) # Column names

str(data) # Structure of data

summary(data) # Summary statistics
```

When working with data frames (tables), you can use the $ operator to access specific columns by name. For example, data$price refers to the "price" column inside the dataset, letting you analyze or plot that specific variable.

In R, functions are individual commands or tools that perform specific tasks, such as calculating a mean or creating a plot. On the other hand, packages are collections of related functions and datasets bundled together to extend R's capabilities. Think of packages as toolkits or libraries that you install and load when you want extra features beyond base R. For example, the ggplot2 package contains many functions specifically designed for advanced data visualization.

After loading and exploring data, you often use functions to create simple visualizations or calculate basic statistics. For example, plot() creates a scatterplot, hist() creates a histogram, and mean() calculates the average value of a variable. Here are some examples:

R Code
```
# Create simple plots


# Scatter plot of price vs. quantity
plot(data$price, data$quantity)


hist(data$price) # Histogram of price


# Basic statistics


mean(data$price) # Mean price


median(data$price) # Median price


table(data$category) # Frequency count of categories
```

Part 6: Tips for Success

Set Your Working Directory

In R, the working directory is the folder on your computer where R looks for files to read and where it saves files by default. It's important to set your working directory to the location where your data files are stored so that you can easily load and save files without typing long file paths. You can set the working directory in R using the setwd() function with the path to your folder, for example:

R Code
```
setwd("C:/Users/YourName/Documents/DataMining").
```

Alternatively, if you're using RStudio, you can set it through the menu by going to the menu bar and Session → Set Working Directory → Choose Directory and selecting the appropriate folder. Setting your working directory correctly helps keep your projects organized and makes working with data files smoother.

File Management

When working in R, it's important to regularly save your progress to avoid losing any of your code or data. The scripts you write in R, which contain your R code, can be saved by pressing Ctrl+S on Windows or Cmd+S on a Mac. These script files usually have the extension .R. Saving your script means your code is safely stored on your computer and can be opened, edited, or run again later without starting from scratch.

Beyond saving scripts, R has something called a workspace, which you can think of as the current memory of your R session. The workspace holds all the data objects, variables, and functions you have created during your work.

Saving the workspace means saving everything you've done so far so that when you come back later, you don't have to reload or recreate all your data and settings — you can pick up exactly where you left off.

To keep everything related to a specific analysis or project organized, RStudio offers a helpful feature called Projects. A project bundles together all your scripts, data files, workspace, and any other documents into a single folder. This way, when you open a project, all the files and information you need for that particular task are in one place. This organization is especially useful if you are working on multiple assignments or analyses at the same time because it prevents files from getting mixed up or lost.

You can create a new project easily in RStudio by going to File → New Project. Using projects helps make your workflow smoother and your work more manageable. So, in summary, regularly save your .R scripts to keep your code safe, save your workspace to keep your data and variables intact, and use RStudio projects to keep everything related to your work well-organized.

Getting Help

When you're working in R, it's common to need help understanding what a function does or how to use it. A strength of R is the well written internal help support system. One way to get help is by typing commands directly in the Console. For example, if you want to learn about the mean() function, you can type ?mean and press Enter, and R will show the documentation for that function. Similarly, if you want to search for help on a topic or keyword, like "clustering," you can type ??clustering to find all related help pages.

In addition to these commands, RStudio provides a very useful Help pane located in the bottom-right corner of the interface. This Help pane allows you to search for functions, packages, and topics without needing to remember the exact commands. You can simply type a keyword or function name into the search box, and relevant help files and guides will appear for you to browse. Clicking on any of these entries will open detailed documentation, including examples of how to use the function, explanations of its arguments, and additional resources.

Using both the help commands (? and ??) in the Console and the Help pane in RStudio gives you quick and easy access to the information you need, making it much easier to learn and troubleshoot as you work with R.

Common Errors and Solutions

As you run script in R the Console will have error messages. Get familiar with what these mean in case you need to trouble shoot.

Error: "Object not found"

  • Solution: Make sure you've run the code that creates the object

  • Check spelling and capitalization (R is case-sensitive)

Error: "Package not found"

  • Solution: Install the package first with install.packages("packagename")

Error: "Cannot find file"

  • Solution: Check your working directory and file path

  • Use getwd() to see current directory

Best Practices for Script Users

When working with scripts, start by reading the comments—these are lines beginning with # that often explain what each part of the code does. Avoid running the entire script all at once right away; instead, run it section by section to better understand how it works and catch errors early. As you go, check the Environment pane to confirm that variables and objects are being created as expected. Keep your data files well-organized by placing them in the same folder as your scripts, which helps avoid file path issues. Finally, always make a backup copy of the original script before making any changes, so you can easily revert if needed.

Lab 2

Vectors and Basic Data Types

In this lab, you will learn about vectors, one of the fundamental data structures in R. Vectors are one-dimensional arrays that store elements of the same data type. Understanding vectors is essential as vectors are the building blocks for more complex data structures in R, such as data frames.

We will explore four common types of vectors: numeric, character, logical, and factor (categorical). By the end of this lab, you will be comfortable creating vectors, inspecting their contents, and checking their data types.

Lesson Steps

Step 1: Create Vectors

Let's start by creating four vectors, each representing a different data type:

R Code
```
# Numeric vector (numbers)
ages <- c(25, 30, 22, 28)


# Character vector (text)
names <- c("Alice", "Bob", "Carol", "David")


# Logical vector (TRUE or FALSE)
passed <- c(TRUE, FALSE, TRUE, TRUE)


# Factor vector (categorical data with fixed levels)
genders <- factor(c("Female", "Male", "Female", "Male"))
```

Step 2: Print Vectors

To see what you have stored in these vectors, print them on the console:

R Code
```
# Print vectors
print(ages)
```

Output
```
## [1] 25 30 22 28
```

R Code
```
print(names)
```

Output
```
## [1] "Alice" "Bob"    "Carol" "David"
```

R Code
```
print(passed)
```

Output
```
## [1]   TRUE FALSE   TRUE   TRUE
```

R Code
```
print(genders)
```

Output
```
## [1] Female Male    Female Male
## Levels: Female Male
```

Step 3: Understanding the `class()` Function

In R, every object has a class, which tells R what type of data it is dealing with. The class() function returns the class (i.e., the data type) of an object. This is important because different functions in R behave differently depending on an object's class.

For example: - Numbers are treated as `numeric` - Text is treated as `character` - TRUE/FALSE values are `logical` - Categorical values are stored as `factor`

Let's look at how this works using the vectors we created earlier:

R Code
```
# Check the class of each vector
class(ages)    # Should return "numeric"
```

Output
```
## [1] "numeric"
```

R Code
```
class(names)    # Should return "character"
```

Output
```
## [1] "character"
```

R Code
```
class(passed)   # Should return "logical"
```

Output
```
## [1] "logical"
```

R Code
```
class(genders) # Should return "factor"
```

Output
```
## [1] "factor"
```

When you run class(ages), R returns "numeric" because ages is a vector of numbers. Similarly, names is a character vector, passed is a logical vector (TRUE/FALSE), and genders is a factor, which R uses to represent categorical data.

Understanding the class of a vector is important because it determines how R will treat the data in calculations, visualizations, and other operations. Misclassified data types can cause issues. This is especially crucial when combining vectors into more complex structures like data frames.

Wrap-Up

Vectors are a foundational data structure in R. They hold elements of the same type such as numbers, text, logical values, or categorical factors. Knowing how to create and inspect vectors is critical.

Exercises

Vectors and Basic Data Types

In this exercise set, you will practice creating and inspecting different types of vectors: numeric, character, logical, and factor. For each dataset, read the description, create the vectors in R, and answer the follow-up questions using print() and class() as learned in Lab 1-1.

Pet Preferences

```
R Code
# Numeric vector: number of pets owned
num_pets <- c(2, 0, 3, 1)

# Character vector: student names
students <- c("Liam", "Mia", "Noah", "Ava")

# Logical vector: owns a dog
owns_dog <- c(TRUE, FALSE, TRUE, FALSE)

# Factor vector: favorite type of pet
favorite_pet <- factor(c("Dog", "Cat", "Dog", "Bird"))
```

1. Use print() to display each vector.

2. What is the class of each vector? Use class() to find out.

3. Which vector stores TRUE/FALSE values? Which stores text?

4. What class is favorite_pet, and why is it useful?

5. How can you tell that `num_pets` is numeric?

Online Course Participation

This dataset represents four students enrolled in an online course. For each student, we record how many hours they spent studying, their username, whether they completed the first quiz, and their preferred learning style. Each type of data is stored in its appropriate vector format for analysis.

```
R Code
# Numeric vector: hours spent on course
study_hours <- c(5, 3, 8, 2)

# Character vector: usernames
usernames <- c("datafan", "codequeen", "rlearner", "statstar")

# Logical vector: completed first quiz
quiz_done <- c(TRUE, TRUE, FALSE, FALSE)

# Factor vector: preferred learning style
learning_style <- factor(c("Visual", "Auditory",
                           "Visual", "Reading"))
```

6. Print each vector to see its contents.

7. What class is each vector? Use the `class()` function.

8. Which vector could be used in a mathematical calculation? Why?

9. What kind of data is stored in `quiz_done`?

10. What does `class(learning_style)` return, and what does that tell you?

Lab 3

Creating and Exploring Data Frames in R

Data frames are one of the most important data structures in R. The structure of a data frame is like a spreadsheet: it has rows and columns, where each column is a variable and each row is an observation. Each column can hold a different type of data—such as numbers, text, or TRUE/FALSE values—but all the values within a column must be the same type.

In this lesson, you'll learn how to combine multiple vectors into a single data frame, creating a structured table of data. You'll also examine the structure and summary statistics of the data frame to better understand your data set. Finally, you'll learn how to access specific columns, rows, and individual elements within the data frame for analysis and manipulation

Lesson Steps

Step 1: Create a Data Frame

We begin by combining four vectors—names, ages, passed, and genders—into a data frame.

```
R Code
# Numeric vector (numbers)
ages <- c(25, 30, 22, 28)


# Character vector (text)
names <- c("Alice", "Bob", "Carol", "David")


# Logical vector (TRUE or FALSE)
passed <- c(TRUE, FALSE, TRUE, TRUE)


# Factor vector (categorical data with fixed levels)
genders <- factor(c("Female", "Male", "Female", "Male"))



# Create a data frame from the vectors
df <- data.frame(Name = names,
                 Age = ages,
                 Passed = passed,
                 Gender = genders)
```

Each vector becomes a column in the data frame. The Name column contains
names stored as character data. The Age column holds numeric values representing ages. The Passed column contains logical values indicating TRUE
or FALSE. Finally, the Gender column stores categorical values as a factor.

Step 2: View the Full Data Frame

The print() function is used to display the entire data frame in the R console.
When you call print(df), it shows all the rows and columns of the data frame,
providing a view of the complete table of data. This is useful for quickly
inspecting your dataset to verify that it looks as expected.

R Code
```
# Print the entire data frame
print(df)
```

Output
```
##      Name Age Passed Gender
## 1 Alice   25    TRUE Female
## 2   Bob   30   FALSE   Male
## 3 Carol   22    TRUE Female
## 4 David   28    TRUE   Male
```

Step 3: Examine the Structure with str()

Function str()provides a compact and informative summary of your data frame's internal structure. It shows you how many observations (rows) and variables (columns) the data frame contains. It also reveals the data type of each column (such as numeric, factor, or logical) and gives a preview of the first few values in each column.

R Code
```
# Get structure and data types
str(df)
```

Output
```
## 'data.frame':    4 obs. of  4 variables:
##  $ Name  : chr  "Alice" "Bob" "Carol" "David"
##  $ Age   : num  25 30 22 28
##  $ Passed: logi  TRUE FALSE TRUE TRUE
##  $ Gender: Factor w/ 2 levels "Female","Male": 1 2 1 2
```

Step 4: Get Summary Statistics

The summary() function provides a quick overview of the contents of your data frame by calculating summary statistics for each column. For numeric columns, it shows statistics like the minimum, maximum, mean, and quartiles. For categorical or factor columns, it gives counts of each category or level. For logical columns, it summarizes how many values are TRUE or FALSE. This concise report makes viewing data easier to spot trends or anomalies.

R Code
```
# Summary statistics for numeric columns
summary(df[, c("Age")])
```

Output
```
##    Min. 1st Qu.  Median    Mean 3rd Qu.    Max.
##   22.00   24.25   26.50   26.25   28.50   30.00
```

R Code
```
# Summary statistics for non-numeric columns
summary(df[, c("Name", "Passed", "Gender")])
```

Output
```
##       Name              Passed           Gender
##   Length:4          Mode :logical    Female:2
##   Class :character  FALSE:1          Male  :2
##   Mode  :character  TRUE :3
```

The output of summary() shows the minimum, mean, and maximum values for numeric columns. For logical columns, it provides counts of TRUE and FALSE values. For factor columns, it displays the number of occurrences for each category or level.

Step 5: Access Columns

In a data frame, each column has a label, called its name (like "Age" or "Name"), which describes what kind of data it holds and is set by the user. Columns are also arranged in a specific order, so each one has a position number called its index (for example, the first column has index 1, the second column has index 2, and so on). You can access, or select, a column either by using its name (the label) or by its position number in the data frame. This lets you work with just the parts of the data you need.

R Code
```
# By name
df$Age
```

Output
```
## [1] 25 30 22 28
```

R Code
```
# By index (2nd column)
df[[2]]
```

Output
```
## [1] 25 30 22 28
```

R Code
```
# Select multiple columns by name or index
df[c("Name", "Gender")]
```

Output
```
##     Name Gender
## 1 Alice Female
## 2   Bob   Male
## 3 Carol Female
## 4 David   Male
```

R Code
```
df[c(1, 4)]
```

Output
```
##     Name Gender
## 1 Alice Female
## 2   Bob   Male
## 3 Carol Female
## 4 David   Male
```

These commands show different ways to select columns from a data frame. Using df$Age accesses the column named "Age" directly by its name. The notation df[[2]] selects the second column by its position number, or index, in the data frame. To select multiple columns at once, you can provide their names as a vector with df[c("Name", "Gender")] or their positions with df[c(1, 4)]. This flexibility allows you to easily extract one or more columns based on what you find most convenient, either by the column's label or by where it appears in the data frame.

Step 6: Access Rows

Accessing rows by their number allows you to select specific observations or groups of observations from your data frame. Since each row represents one case or record in your dataset, specifying row numbers lets you focus on entries for inspection, analysis, or modification. By using the row's position—like the 3rd row or rows 1 through 3—you can quickly retrieve those observations and work with just that subset of data. This is helpful when you want to examine example cases, check data quality, or perform operations on selected rows.

R Code
```
# Select the 3rd row
df[3, ]
```

Output
```
##      Name Age Passed Gender
## 3 Carol  22    TRUE Female
```

R Code
```
# Select multiple rows (1st to 3rd)
df[1:3, ]
```

Output
```
##      Name Age Passed Gender
## 1 Alice  25    TRUE Female
## 2   Bob  30   FALSE   Male
## 3 Carol  22    TRUE Female
```

Accessing rows by their number lets you inspect specific observations in your dataset. By specifying the row number, you can look at the data for specific entries, which is useful for checking details, finding errors, or focusing your analysis on certain entries.

Step 7: Access Individual Elements

To examine or work with a single value in your data frame, you can specify both its row and column. This lets you pinpoint exactly one cell by indicating which observation (row) and which variable (column) you want to access, using the notation [row, column].

```
R Code
# Value in 2nd row, 3rd column
df[2, 3]
```

```
Output
## [1] FALSE
```

```
R Code
# Value in 4th row, "Name" column
df[4, "Name"]
```

```
Output
## [1] "David"
```

This approach lets you precisely extract or change a single value within your data frame. It's helpful when you need to focus on one specific piece of data—for example, correcting a mistake, checking an individual measurement, or using that value in a calculation—without affecting the rest of the dataset.

Wrap-Up

Data frames are fundamental tools for working with real-world data in R. They provide a structured way to organize and examine datasets, making it easier to analyze patterns, clean and filter information, and prepare data for visualizations or statistical models. Mastering how to create, explore, and access data frames is an essential for effective in data analysis with R.

Exercises

Creating and Exploring Data Frames

Here you will apply what you learned in the lab to explore and manipulate data frames. You'll start by creating a data frame from multiple vectors, then investigate its structure and content using built-in R functions.

Dataset 1: Student Performance Data

```
R Code
# Vectors for student data
ages <- c(19, 24, 21, 23)
names <- c("Maya", "Liam", "Noah", "Zoe")
passed <- c(FALSE, TRUE, TRUE, FALSE)
genders <- factor(c("Female", "Male", "Male",
                    "Female"))


# Combine into a data frame
df <- data.frame(Name = names,
                 Age = ages,
                 Passed = passed,
                 Gender = genders)
```

1. Use `print(df)` to display the full data frame. Paste the output. What does each row represent?

2. Use `str(df)` to examine the structure of the data frame. What are the data types of each column?

3. Use `summary(df)` to generate summary statistics.

   - What is the average (mean) age?

- How many students passed?

4. Use column access methods to answer:

    - What are the values in the `Age` column?
    - What is the second method you can use to get the same result?

5. Use row access to answer:

    - What are the values in the third row?
    - How would you extract just the name from that row?

Dataset 2: Course Satisfaction Survey

```
R Code
# Vectors for survey data
names2 <- c("Emily", "Frank", "Grace", "Hank")
ratings <- c(4.5, 3.8, 5.0, 4.2)
recommend <- c(TRUE, FALSE, TRUE, TRUE)
majors <- factor(c("Biology", "Math", "Biology",
                   "Physics"))

# Combine into a data frame
survey <- data.frame(Name = names2,
                     Rating = ratings,
                     Recommend = recommend,
                     Major = majors)
```

6. What is the structure of the `survey` data frame? Use `str()` and paste the result.

7. Use `summary(survey)` to summarize the data.

    - What is the minimum and maximum course rating?

- Which major appears most frequently?

8. Use indexing to access:

    - The name of the third student
    - Whether the second student would recommend the course

9. Access a single value:

    - What is the course rating for the fourth student?
    - What is that student's major?

10. Use indexing to retrieve only the `Name` and `Rating` columns. What are their values?

Lab 4

Tibbles and the Tidyverse

Tidyverse is a powerful set of R packages that simplify data science with consistent, readable syntax. It includes tools and packages for data manipulation, visualization, and tidying, and features an improved type of data frame called a Tibble. Tibbles organize data in rows and columns like traditional data frames but offer enhancements that improve usability and integration with Tidyverse packages. Tidyverse packages can be bundle downloaded (which installs but does not load all packages for use but will load a core of packages) or separate element packages may be individually installed and loaded.

In this lab, you will learn what Tidyverse is and why it's useful, understand the differences between traditional data frames and Tibbles, and create a Tibble to compare it with a regular data frame.

Lesson Steps

Step 1: Understand Tibbles

A core element of the tidyverse is the Tibble, a replacement for the traditional data frame. Unlike data frames, Tibbles don't convert strings to factors automatically, preventing common pitfalls of string data becoming a factor when it shoul dnot. They also print more cleanly in the console by showing only a concise preview of the data, especially helpful for large datasets. Tibbles integrate seamlessly with other Tidyverse tools like dplyr and ggplot2 as the tidyverse packages are designed to work together.

Step 2: Install and Load the Tibble Package

Before you can use a package, you need to install it on your computer and then load it into your R session. Installing a package means downloading it from the internet and saving it on your computer. You only need to do this once for each package (assuming you use the same computer and setup).

Loading a package means telling R to make the package's functions available to use in your current work session. You need to do this every time you start a new R session and want to use the package.

To install the Tibble package, run this command once:

```
R Code
install.packages("tibble")
```

This downloads and installs the package. But function library() loads the package making it available to use in the current work session (without do- ing this only base R functionality is in the work session).

```
R Code
library(tibble)
```

After loading, you can use the functions provided by the package.

Step 3: Create a Tibble

To create a tibble, start by defining vectors that store your data. Then combine these vectors into a tibble, which organizes your data in a clean, structured format ideal for analysis with Tidyverse tools.

```
R Code
# Vectors of data
names <- c("Alice", "Bob", "Carol", "David")
ages <- c(25, 30, 22, 28)
passed <- c(TRUE, FALSE, TRUE, TRUE)
genders <- factor(c("Female", "Male", "Female", "Male"))


# Combine vectors in tibble
tb <- tibble(
  Name = names,
  Age = ages,
  Passed = passed,
  Gender = genders
)
```

Step 4: Compare Tibbles and Data Frames

Now, create a traditional data frame using the same vectors and print both the data frame and the tibble. This comparison will show how Tibbles provide cleaner, more readable console output compared to traditional data frames.

R Code

```
# Create a traditional data frame
# Use vectors created above
df <- data.frame(
  Name = names,
  Age = ages,
  Passed = passed,
  Gender = genders
)


# Print the traditional data frame
print(df)
```

Output

```
##     Name Age Passed Gender
## 1 Alice  25   TRUE Female
## 2   Bob  30  FALSE   Male
## 3 Carol  22   TRUE Female
## 4 David  28   TRUE   Male
```

R Code

```
# Print the tibble
print(tb)
```

Output

```
## # A tibble: 4 x 4
##    Name    Age Passed Gender
##    <chr> <dbl> <lgl>  <fct>
## 1 Alice    25 TRUE   Female
## 2 Bob      30 FALSE  Male
## 3 Carol    22 TRUE   Female
## 4 David    28 TRUE   Male
```

Step 5: Check the Object Classes

To understand the difference between a traditional data frame and a tibble, use the `class()` function. This shows the underlying object types. It will confirm that while both share similarities, Tibbles have additional classes that enable their enhanced features.

R Code

```
class(df)  # Outputs: "data.frame"
```

Output

```
## [1] "data.frame"
```

R Code

```
class(tb)  # Outputs: "tbl_df" "tbl" "data.frame"
```

Output
```
## [1] "tbl_df"      "tbl"          "data.frame"
```

When you use class() on a tibble, it returns multiple classes like "tbl_df", "tbl", and "data.frame". This happens because a tibble is built as an extension (object inheritance in programming lingo) of a traditional data frame ("data.frame"), but with additional features provided by the "tbl" and "tbl_df" classes. These extra classes allow Tibbles to behave like data frames while also supporting enhanced printing, better subsetting, and smoother integration with Tidyverse functions. Tibbles have additional special behaviors without losing compatibility with data frames.

Wrap-Up

In this lesson, you learned about Tidyverse and how it introduces Tibbles as an improved alternative to traditional data frames. You practiced creating Tibbles from vectors and saw how their cleaner console output and special object classes make data exploration easier and more intuitive.

Exercises

Tibbles and the Tidyverse

These exercises will help you practice using tibbles and explore the differences between tibbles and traditional data frames. You will create both types, compare their outputs, and examine how they behave in R.

Dataset: Student Information Tibble

```
R Code
# Vectors for student data
ages <- c(19, 24, 21, 23)
names <- c("Maya", "Liam", "Noah", "Zoe")
passed <- c(FALSE, TRUE, TRUE, FALSE)
genders <- factor(c("Female", "Male", "Male",
                    "Female"))

# Combine vectors in tibble
tb <- tibble(
Name = names,
Age = ages,
Passed = passed,
Gender = genders
)
```

1. Print the tibble. What do you notice about the way the tibble displays in the console compared to a data frame?

2. What are the classes of the `tb` object? Use `class(tb)` and paste the output. How is this different from a traditional data frame?

3. Use the `str()` function on the tibble. How many rows and columns are there? What are the types of the variables?

4. Use the `summary()` function on the tibble. What is the average age? How many students passed?

5. Extract the `Name` and `Passed` columns from the tibble. Paste the R code you used and describe the result.

Traditional Data Frame (Same Data)

```
R Code
# Create a traditional data frame from the same vectors
df <- data.frame(
  Name = names,
  Age = ages,
  Passed = passed,
  Gender = genders
)
```

6. Use `print(df)` and compare it with `print(tb)`. How are they different in appearance and formatting?

7. What class does the object `df` belong to? Use `class(df)`.

8. What happens when you use `str(df)`? Does it show the same information as `str(tb)`? Which format is easier to read?

9. Use indexing to extract the second row from `df`. Paste the output. Now try the same with `tb[2, ]`. Are the results the same?

10. Extract the `Gender` column using $ from both `df` and `tb`. Are the results identical? Paste your code and output.

Lab 5

Structured vs. Unstructured Data

In data analytics, understanding the difference between structured and unstructured data is crucial. Structured data is highly organized, usually stored in rows and columns like a spreadsheet or database table, making it easy to search, filter, and analyze. In R, structured data is stored in data frames or Tibbles, where each column represents a variable and each row represents an observation.

Unstructured data, on the other hand, has no fixed format. It includes text, emails, images, or audio. This data is more flexible but requires special processing for analysis. In R, unstructured data is usually stored in character vectors or other specialized data structures depending on the content.

Lesson Steps

Step 1: Create and View Structured Data

Structured data is organized into clear rows and columns. Here's how to create a simple structured data frame in R:

R Code

```
structured_data <- data.frame(
  ID = 1:3,
  Name = c("A", "B", "C"),
  Score = c(90, 85, 88)
)

print(structured_data)
```

Output

```
##    ID Name Score
## 1  1    A    90
## 2  2    B    85
## 3  3    C    88
```

This creates a table with three rows and three columns, making it easy to perform analyses like sorting or filtering.

Step 2: Create and View Unstructured Data

Unstructured data refers to information that does not have a predefined or organized format like rows and columns. This includes text documents, emails, social media posts, images, audio, video, and more. Unlike structured data, which fits neatly into tables, unstructured data is often messy and complex but contains valuable insights.

In analytics and AI, unstructured data is increasingly important because much of the information generated today—such as customer reviews, tweets, or sensor data—is unstructured. Techniques like natural language processing (NLP), image recognition, and speech analysis are used to extract meaning from unstructured data and make it usable for decision-making, predictions, and automation.

In R, unstructured text data is typically stored as character vectors. Here's a simple example:

```
R Code
unstructured_text <- c(
  "This is a first sentence.",
  "Here is another line of text.",
  "Data science deals with unstructured data too."
)
```

This kind of data requires different techniques for processing and analysis compared to structured data.

Step 3: Simple Processing of Unstructured Data

Unstructured data needs special methods for analysis because it lacks a fixed format. For example, when working with text data, you can convert all text to lowercase to standardize it. You might count the number of words or sentences to get a sense of its length or complexity. Searching for specific keywords helps identify important information within the text. These simple preprocessing steps prepare unstructured data for more advanced analysis in data science and AI.

Here's a basic example converting text to lowercase and counting words:

R Code
```
# Set R's output width
options(width = 40)


# Sample unstructured text
text <- c("Data Science is FUN!",
          "Unstructured data needs processing.")


# Convert to lowercase
text_lower <- tolower(text)


# Count words in each element
word_counts <- sapply(strsplit(text_lower, " "),
                      length)


print(text_lower)
```

Output
```
## [1] "data science is fun!"
## [2] "unstructured data needs processing."
```

R Code
```
print(word_counts)
```

Output
```
## [1] 4 4
```

Wrap-Up

In this lesson, you explored the difference between structured and unstructured data. You practiced creating examples of both in R using data frames for structured data and character vectors for unstructured data.

Exercises

Structured vs. Unstructured Data

These exercises will help you explore and understand the differences between structured and unstructured data by working with both in R. You'll create your own data sets, apply simple processing steps, and reflect on how the data structure affects analysis methods.

Part 1: Structured Data

Use the following code to create a structured data frame:

```
R Code
structured_data <- data.frame(
  ID = 101:103,
  Name = c("Jasper", "Nina", "Leo"),
  Score = c(72, 95, 83)
)
```

1. What type of R object is `structured_data`? Use the `class()` function to find out.

2. Use `str(structured_data)` to examine the structure. How many rows and columns does the data frame have?

3. Use indexing to extract the second row. Paste your code and the result.

4. Extract just the `Score` column using the $ operator. What are the values?

5. Calculate the average score using `mean()`. Paste your code and the result.

Part 2: Unstructured Data

Use the code below to define a simple character vector representing unstructured text data.

```
R Code
unstructured_text <- c(
  "Weather was unexpectedly warm today.",
  "Cats often nap in strange places.",
  "Learning R can be both fun and frustrating.",
  "Books piled high covered the old desk.",
  "A sudden knock startled everyone in the room."
)
```

6. What type of R object is `unstructured_text`? Use the `class()` function.

7. How many separate text entries are in the `unstructured_text` vector? Use `length()`.

8. Use `tolower(unstructured_text)` to convert all the text to lowercase. What is the output?

9. Use `strsplit(unstructured_text, " ")` to split the text into words. How many words are in the first sentence? (Use `length()`)

Simple Text Processing

```
R Code
# Sample unstructured text
text <- c("Sunsets are truly magical.",
          "Reading opens up new worlds.")

# Convert to lowercase
text_lower <- tolower(text)

# Count words
word_counts <- sapply(strsplit(text_lower, " "),
                      length)
```

10. What does `tolower()` do, and why is it useful when working with un-structured text?

11. What are the two elements of `text_lower` after conversion?

12. How many words are in each sentence?   Use the output from `word_counts`.

13. Think about real-world data:

    • Give one example of structured data you've seen.
    • Give one example of unstructured data you've seen.
    • Which one do you think is easier to analyze, and why?

Lab 6

Descriptive Statistics

When beginning an analysis on new data it's important first to get a sense of the data. Descriptive statistics help you summarize and interpret the main features of a dataset. In this lab, you'll learn how to calculate and understand measures of central tendency such as the mean, median, and mode. You'll also explore measures of variability, including standard deviation, variance, and range.

Lesson Steps

Step 1: Load Basic Tools

We'll use two R packages to help us work with the data. First, we'll load the Tidyverse. It includes tools like dplyr for data wrangling and ggplot2 for plotting, and it uses consistent, beginner-friendly syntax. Second, we'll load the modeest package. This package allows us to calculate the mode of a data set. Unlike the mean or median, R does not have a built-in function for calculating the mode (which is odd and not logical).

R Code
```
# Install if not already installed
options(repos = c(CRAN = "https://cran.r-project.org"))
install.packages("tidyverse")
install.packages("modeest")


# Load libraries
library(tidyverse)
library(modeest)
```

Step 2: Create Example Data

Let's create a simple dataset representing the number of items users clicked on during a shopping session.

R Code
```
clicks <- c(1, 1, 2, 2, 2, 3, 3, 4, 10, 15)

print(clicks)
```

Output
```
##  [1]  1  1  2  2  2  3  3  4 10 15
```

Step 3: Measures of Central Tendency

To understand the center of a dataset, we often look at the mean, median, and mode. These measures help us describe where most values lie and provide insight into the typical experience or outcome. Let's apply each measure to a sample vector of user click data.

Mean

The mean is the average of all values.

```
R Code
mean(clicks)
```

```
Output
## [1] 4.3
```

The mean number of clicks, calculated with mean(clicks), is 4.3, indicating that on average users clicked about 4 items, though this average is influenced by a few high values.

Median

The median is the middle value when the data is sorted least to greatest value.

```
R Code
median(clicks)
```

```
Output
## [1] 2.5
```

The median, found using median(clicks), is 2.5, meaning half of the clicks are below and half above this value, which better represents a typical user when the data contains outliers.

Mode

The mode is the most frequently occurring value. We'll use mlv() from the modeest package.

```
R Code
mlv(clicks, method = "mfv")
```

```
Output
## [1] 2
```

Finally, the mode, estimated with mlv(clicks, method = "mfv") from the modeest package, is 2, showing that 2 clicks is the most common number among users in this dataset.

Step 4: Measures of Dispersion

Dispersion measures tell us how spread out the values in a dataset are around the center (usually the mean) and help us understand the variability or consistency in the data.

Variance and standard deviation

Variance and standard deviation both measure how spread out the values in a dataset are from the mean, but they differ in how that spread is expressed. Variance calculates the average of the squared differences between each data point and the mean, giving a measure in squared units (which is often not desirable to interpret since the original data is not squared). Standard deviation is the square root of the variance, which converts the spread back into the original units of the data, making it easier to interpret.

R Code
```
sd(clicks)
```

Output
```
## [1] 4.571652
```

R Code
```
var(clicks)
```

Output
```
## [1] 20.9
```

The standard deviation shows, on average, how far data points deviate from the mean; in our dataset, it is about 4.57, meaning clicks typically vary by roughly 4.57 from the average of 4.3 clicks. Variance is the square of the standard deviation and represents the average squared deviation from the mean; here, it's 20.9, which is less intuitive but useful in some calculations.

Range

Range tells us the smallest and largest values in the dataset.

R Code
```
range(clicks)
```

Output
```
## [1]  1 15
```

The range simply shows the minimum and maximum values—in this case, clicks range from 1 to 15. The range highlights the spread between the smallest and largest observations.

Coefficient of variation

The Coefficient of Variation (CV) is the ratio of the standard deviation to the mean, expressed as a percentage. It gives a relative measure of dispersion regardless of the unit of measurement and is calculated as:

R Code
```
cv <- sd(clicks) / mean(clicks) * 100
cv
```

Output
```
## [1] 106.3175
```

Step 5: Summary Statistics

The summary() function in R provides a quick overview of the main characteristics of your data, but its output depends on the type of object it is applied to. When used on a numeric vector, summary() returns key statistics such as the minimum, first quartile, median, mean, third quartile, and maximum values. These statistics give you a concise understanding of the data's center, spread, and range.

For example, applying summary() to a vector of click counts shows you the smallest and largest number of clicks, the middle value, and the average clicks, helping you grasp the overall distribution.

R Code
```
summary(clicks)
```

Output
```
##     Min. 1st Qu.  Median    Mean 3rd Qu.
##     1.00    2.00    2.50    4.30    3.75
##     Max.
##    15.00
```

Wrap-Up

Descriptive statistics provide an essential first look at your data. By calculating the mean, median, and mode, you can understand the central tendency of your data. Measures like standard deviation and range help reveal how spread out the values are. These insights form the foundation for more advanced data analysis.

Exercises

Descriptive Statistics

In this exercise, you will explore key descriptive statistics used to summarize data.

Dataset 1: Click Counts

```
R Code
clicks <- c(2, 5, 5, 6, 8, 12, 20)
```

1. What is the mean number of clicks?

2. What is the median number of clicks?

3. What is the mode of the dataset?

4. What is the standard deviation and variance of this dataset?

5. Use the `summary()` function. What does the output tell you about the distribution?

Dataset 2: Daily Step Counts

```
R Code
steps <- c(8450, 9020, 7230, 12000, 15000, 10200,
           9500, 11100, 5000, 6100)
```

6. What is the range of this dataset?

7. What is the coefficient of variation (CV) for this dataset?

8. Which measure—mean or median—better represents the typical daily

step count?

9. What does the `summary()` function reveal about this dataset?

10. Are there any unusually high or low values?

Lab 7

Probability, Distributions and Bayes Theorem

Probability is the language of uncertainty, and it plays a central role in data science and machine learning. In this lab, you'll explore key probability distributions—including the normal and Bernoulli. You'll also learn Bayes' Theorem, a powerful probability tool for updating beliefs based on new information.

Lesson Steps

Step 1: Load Libraries

To begin, we'll load the `ggplot2` package, which is part of the tidyverse. This package is ideal for creating clean and customizable plots that help visualize distributions clearly. No other packages are required for this tutorial.

```
R Code
# Install if not already installed
options(repos = c(CRAN = "https://cran.r-project.org"))
install.packages('ggplot2')
library(ggplot2)
```

Step 2: Normal Distribution

The normal distribution—also known as the Gaussian distribution (although for some reason this has gone out of fashion) —is one of the most important and widely used probability distributions in statistics and data science. It has a characteristic bell-shaped curve that is symmetric around the mean, meaning most values cluster around the center and fewer values appear as you move further out in either direction. The shape of a normal distribution is defined by two parameters: the mean (which determines the center) and the standard deviation (which controls the spread).

Many real-world quantitative measurable phenomena—such as heights, test scores, or measurement errors—tend to follow a roughly normal distribution. It also forms the basis of many inferential statistical methods, including hypothesis testing.

Let's start by generating a sample of 1000 values from a standard normal distribution (mean = 0, standard deviation = 1), and then visualize it using ggplot2:

```
R Code
# Generate 1000 random values from a normal distribution
normal_data <- rnorm(1000, mean = 0, sd = 1)
```

Next, we'll create a histogram of the values and overlay the theoretical normal density function to compare the empirical and theoretical shapes.

```
R Code
# Plot the distribution
ggplot(data.frame(x = normal_data), aes(x)) +
  geom_histogram(aes(y = ..density..),
    bins = 30, fill = "#98C1D9", color = "black") +
    stat_function(fun = dnorm, args =
    list(mean = 0, sd = 1), color = "#EE6C4D", size = 1) +
    labs(title = "Normal Distribution", x = "Value",
                y = "Density")
```

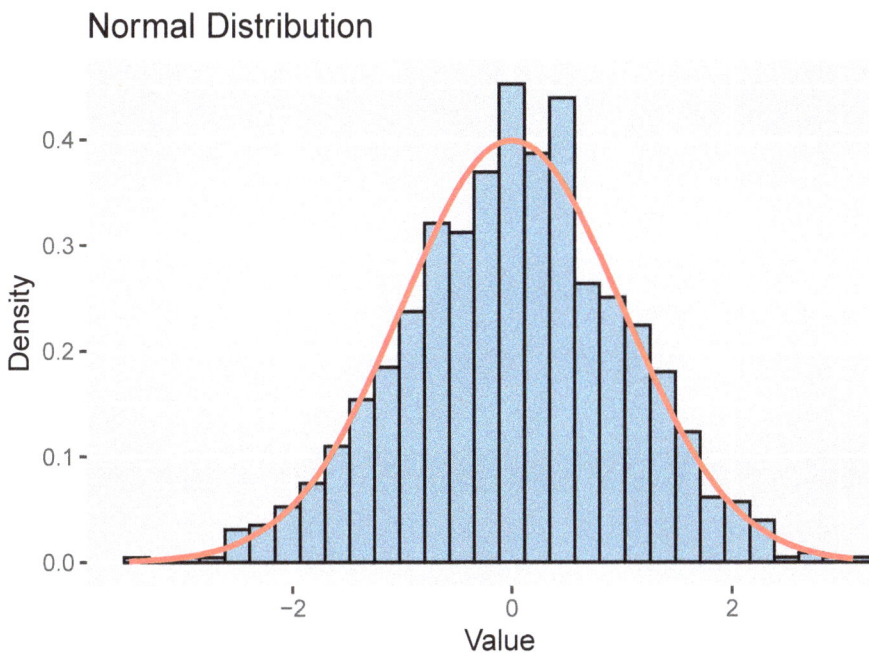

Normal Distribution

The resulting plot shows the classic bell-shaped curve of a normal distribution, where most values are clustered around the mean (0), and fewer values appear as we move away from the center. The line represents the ideal theoretical curve, while the bars show our simulated data.

Step 3: Bernoulli Distribution

The Bernoulli distribution is used to model binary outcomes such as yes/no, success/failure, or fraud/no fraud. It is a core concept behind classification models, including logistic regression.

Let's simulate a simple fraud detection scenario, where each of 1000 transactions has a 10% chance of being fraudulent.

```
R Code
# Simulate 1000 transactions with 10% fraud
set.seed(123)
fraud <- rbinom(n = 1000, size = 1, prob = 0.10)
```

We can check the outcome counts and visualize the distribution using a bar chart.

```
R Code
# View the distribution
table(fraud)
```

```
Output
## fraud
##   0    1
## 908  92
```

R Code

```
# Plot the outcomes
ggplot(data.frame(fraud), aes(x = factor(fraud))) +
  geom_bar(fill = "#637D8D") +
  labs(title = "Bernoulli Distribution - Fraud Detection",
       x = "Outcome (0 = No Fraud, 1 = Fraud)",
       y = "Count")
```

Bernoulli Distribution – Fraud Detection

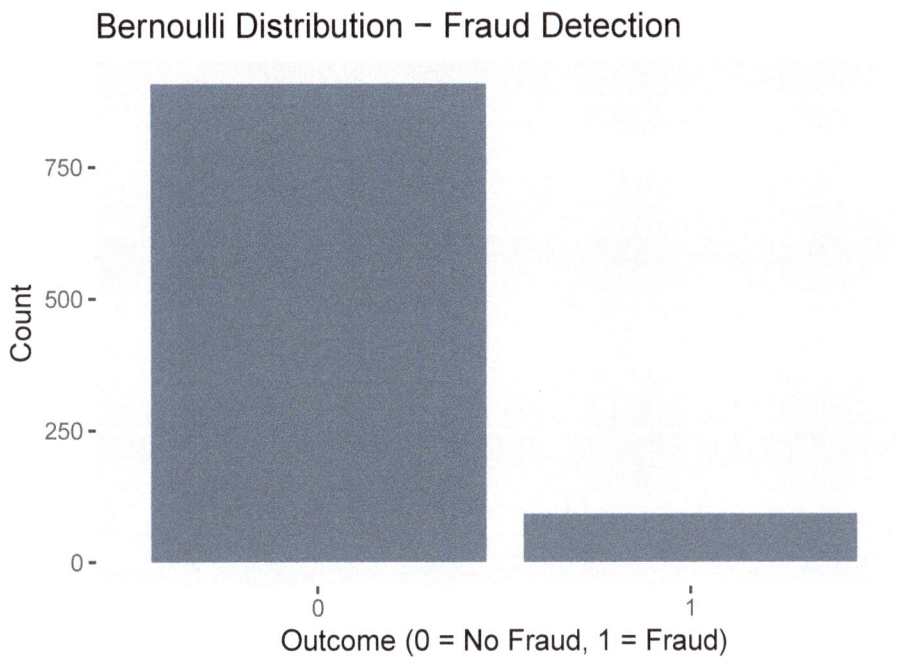

The bar chart displays the typical class imbalance found in real-world datasets. About 10% of the transactions are fraudulent (labeled as 1), and the rest are not. This pattern reflects real-life fraud detection challenges, where positive cases are rare but critically important to detect.

Step 4: Bayes' Theorem Example

Bayes' Theorem allows us to update our probability estimates when we observe new information. In this example, we'll estimate the probability that an email is spam, given that it contains the word "free." Suppose we know that 10% of all emails are spam, 70% of spam emails contain the word "free," and that the word "free" appears in 30% of all emails. We can use Bayes' Theorem to combine these values and calculate the conditional probability.

```
R Code
# Given values
P_H <- 0.10          # P(Spam)
P_E_given_H <- 0.70 # P("Free" | Spam)
P_E <- 0.30          # P("Free")


# Apply Bayes' Theorem
P_H_given_E <- (P_E_given_H * P_H) / P_E


# Display result
cat("P(Spam | 'Free') =", round(P_H_given_E, 4))
```

```
Output
## P(Spam | 'Free') = 0.2333
```

This means that if an email contains the word "free," there is about a 23.33% chance that it is spam. Even though only 10% of all emails are spam, the presence of the word "free" significantly increases the likelihood. This is a powerful demonstration of how Bayes' Theorem helps us revise our beliefs with new evidence, and it is widely used in spam filtering, medical diagnosis, and machine learning applications.

Wrap-Up

In this lab, you explored the role of probability in data science by working with normal and Bernoulli distributions and applying Bayes' Theorem. You visualized a normal distribution and learned how it models natural variation, saw how a Bernoulli distribution captures binary outcomes like fraud detection, and used Bayes' Theorem to update beliefs based on observed data.

Exercises

Probability, Distributions, and Bayes' Theorem

In this exercise you will practice three key concepts in probability and statistics: the normal distribution, the Bernoulli distribution, and Bayes' Theorem.

Dataset 1: Normal Distribution – Exam Scores

This code simulates exam scores for 1,000 students using a normal distribution centered around a mean of 75 with a standard deviation of 8.

```
R Code
set.seed(10)
exam_scores <- rnorm(1000, mean = 75, sd = 8)
```

1. What are the mean and standard deviation of the `exam_scores` vector?

2. What do the `min` and `max` values from `summary(exam_scores)` suggest about score variation?

3. Create a histogram with 25 bins using `ggplot2`. Describe the shape of the distribution.

4. Add a normal curve (density function) to the histogram. How well does the curve fit the histogram?

5. Suppose the passing threshold is 65. What proportion of students scored below that?

Dataset 2: Bernoulli Distribution – Customer Purchases

This code simulates customer purchase behavior for 800 individuals using a Bernoulli distribution with a 25% chance of making a purchase.

```
set.seed(202)
purchases <- rbinom(n = 800, size = 1, prob = 0.25)
```

6. How many customers made a purchase vs. did not?

7. Create a bar chart showing the outcome distribution. What does the visual suggest?

8. Describe whether this distribution is balanced or imbalanced and why that matters.

9. If this were an online store, what would a 25% purchase rate indicate about customer behavior?

10. If the purchase probability changed to 0.50, what change would you expect in the chart?

Dataset 3: Bayes' Theorem – Disease Test Example

Suppose:

- 5% of a population has a rare disease.
- A test detects the disease 95% of the time when it's actually present.
- The test falsely flags healthy people 10% of the time.

Let's use Bayes' Theorem to calculate the probability that a person who tests positive actually has the disease.

```
R Code
P_Disease <- 0.05                # P(Disease)
P_Pos_given_Disease <- 0.95      # P(Positive | Disease)
P_Pos_given_Healthy <- 0.10      # P(Positive | No Disease)


# Calculate P(Positive)
P_Pos <- (P_Pos_given_Disease * P_Disease) +
         (P_Pos_given_Healthy * (1 - P_Disease))


# Apply Bayes' Theorem
P_Disease_given_Pos <- (P_Pos_given_Disease*P_Disease)/
                       P_Pos
```

11. Calculate and report `P_Disease_given_Pos`.

12. In context, interpret what this probability means about a positive test result.

13. If the false positive rate dropped to 5%, how would that affect the final probability?

Lab 8

Correlation and Causality in Data Science

Introduction

Understanding how variables relate to each other is at the heart of data analysis. Correlation is a statistical measure that helps us determine whether—and how strongly—two variables relate. For example, a strong positive correlation means that as one variable increases, the other tends to increase as well. Likewise, a negative correlation means one variable tends to decrease when the other increases. However, it's essential to keep in mind the classic warning in statistics: correlation does not imply causation. Just because two variables move together does not mean that one causes the other.

In this tutorial, you'll explore how to calculate and interpret correlation coefficients using R. You'll learn the difference between Pearson and Spearman correlation metrics and when each is appropriate. Along the way, you'll use ggplot2 to create clear and informative visualizations of relationships between variables. You'll also examine the concept of spurious correlation and causal inference.

Lesson Steps

Step 1: Load Libraries

We'll base R, corplot and the `ggplot2` packages for this lesson.

```
R Code
# Install if not already installed
options(repos = c(CRAN = "https://cran.r-project.org"))
install.packages('ggplot2')
library(ggplot2)


# Optional: load corrplot for visualization
install.packages("corrplot")  # Run this line only once
library(corrplot)
```

Step 2: Simulate Housing Data

We'll create a sample dataset that includes square footage, number of bedrooms, and price, simulating a typical housing dataset.

R Code

```
set.seed(1)
house_data <- data.frame(
  square_feet = rnorm(100, mean = 2000, sd = 300),
  bedrooms = round(rnorm(100, mean = 3, sd = 1)),
  price = rnorm(100, mean = 300000, sd = 50000)
)


# Make price related to square_feet and bedrooms
house_data$price <- 50000 + 100 * house_data$square_feet +
                    20000 * house_data$bedrooms +
                    rnorm(100, 0, 30000)


head(house_data)
```

Output

```
##    square_feet bedrooms    price
## 1    1812.064        2 298016.6
## 2    2055.093        3 284090.4
## 3    1749.311        2 324071.3
## 4    2478.584        3 346349.5
## 5    2098.852        2 349509.6
## 6    1753.859        5 370752.3
```

The command head(house_data) in R shows the first six rows of the house_data dataframe. This is a quick way to preview what your dataset looks like after creation or import.

Note: These are simulated values, so your exact results may vary.

Step 3: Pearson Correlation

The Pearson correlation coefficient measures the linear relationship between two continuous variables.

R Code
```
# Correlation between square feet and price
cor(house_data$square_feet, house_data$price,
    method = "pearson")
```

Output
```
## [1] 0.5856003
```

R Code
```
# Correlation between bedrooms and price
cor(house_data$bedrooms, house_data$price,
    method = "pearson")
```

Output
```
## [1] 0.4184791
```

To better understand the relationship between house size and price, we can use a scatterplot. This type of plot displays individual data points and allows us to visually assess whether there's a pattern or trend. By adding a regression line to the scatterplot, we can see the general direction of the relationship—in this case, whether larger houses tend to sell for more. The plot below uses ggplot2 to graph square footage on the x-axis and price on the y-axis, with a red line representing the best-fitting linear trend.

R Code

```
# Scatterplot with regression line
ggplot(house_data, aes(x = square_feet, y = price)) +
  geom_point(color = "#637D8D") +
  geom_smooth(method = "lm", se = FALSE,
              color = "#EE6C4D") +
  labs(title = "House Price vs. Square Feet",
       x = "Square Feet", y = "Price")
```

House Price vs. Square Feet

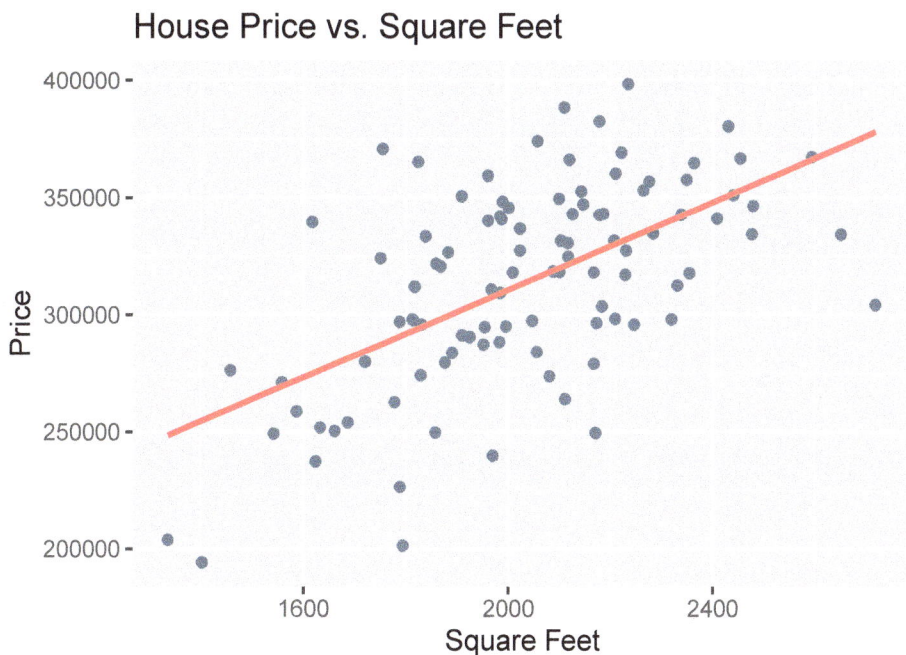

Step 4: Spearman Correlation

While the Pearson correlation measures linear relationships between continuous variables, it assumes that the data follows a roughly straight-line pattern. But what if the relationship is not perfectly linear, yet still consistently increasing or decreasing? This is where Spearman correlation becomes useful.

Spearman correlation does not look at the actual values of the variables—instead, it examines their rank order. It asks: as one variable increases, does the other consistently tend to increase (or decrease), even if not in a perfectly straight line? This makes Spearman ideal for identifying monotonic relationships, where the trend goes steadily up or down without necessarily being linear.

In housing data, for example, the relationship between the number of bedrooms and the price of a home might not be strictly linear. For example, adding a third bedroom might increase the price more than adding a fifth. The Spearman method can still capture that kind of consistent ranking pattern.

R Code
```
# Spearman correlation between bedrooms and price
cor(house_data$bedrooms, house_data$price,
    method = "spearman")
```

Output
```
## [1]  0.4089099
```

Spearman correlation can reveal a pattern of association even when the relationship is not strictly linear. You can also visualize this relationship using a scatterplot. Although the pattern might not form a perfect line, you may still observe a general upward trend in price as the number of bedrooms increases:

R Code

```
# Scatterplot: Bedrooms vs. Price
ggplot(house_data, aes(x = bedrooms, y = price)) +
  geom_point(color = "#3D5A80") +
  geom_smooth(method = "lm", se = FALSE, color = "#EE6C4D") +
  labs(title = "House Price vs. Bedrooms (Spearman)",
       x = "Bedrooms", y = "Price")
```

House Price vs. Bedrooms (Spearman)

Comparing this plot to the earlier one with square footage and Pearson correlation, you may notice that the bedroom–price relationship is more scattered and less linear. That visual inconsistency is exactly why Spearman, which focuses on the ranked positions rather than the actual values, is often the better choice in such cases.

Step 5: Feature Selection Insight

In data science and machine learning, each column in your dataset is referred to as a feature. Features describe specific characteristics of the observations—such as square_feet, bedrooms, or price in a housing dataset. When building predictive models, we want features that provide unique, useful information. However, sometimes multiple features are highly correlated with each other, meaning they convey much of the same information. Including all of them in a model can introduce redundancy, increase computational cost, and even lead to overfitting. For example, if square_feet and bedrooms are very strongly correlated, including both in a model may not be helpful—especially if one of them already captures most of the variance related to the target variable (such as price). In such cases, it's often better to choose just one of the highly correlated features, a process known as feature selection.

Let's explore this further by computing a full correlation matrix of the numerical features in the house_data dataset:

```
R Code
# Compute correlation matrix of numeric features
cor_matrix <- cor(house_data, method = "pearson")
round(cor_matrix, 2)
```

```
Output
##             square_feet bedrooms price
## square_feet        1.00    -0.01  0.59
## bedrooms          -0.01     1.00  0.42
## price              0.59     0.42  1.00
```

This correlation matrix shows how each numeric feature in the dataset is related to the others. Values close to 1 or -1 indicate strong positive or negative correlations, while values near 0 indicate little to no linear relationship.

You can also visualize this correlation matrix to more easily spot highly correlated feature pairs:

R Code
```
# Optional: load corrplot for visualization
install.packages("corrplot")  # Run this line only once
```

Output
```
## Error in install.packages : Updating loaded packages
```

R Code
```
library(corrplot)

# Visualize the correlation matrix
corrplot(cor_matrix, method = "color",
   type = "upper", tl.col = "black", addCoef.col = "black")
```

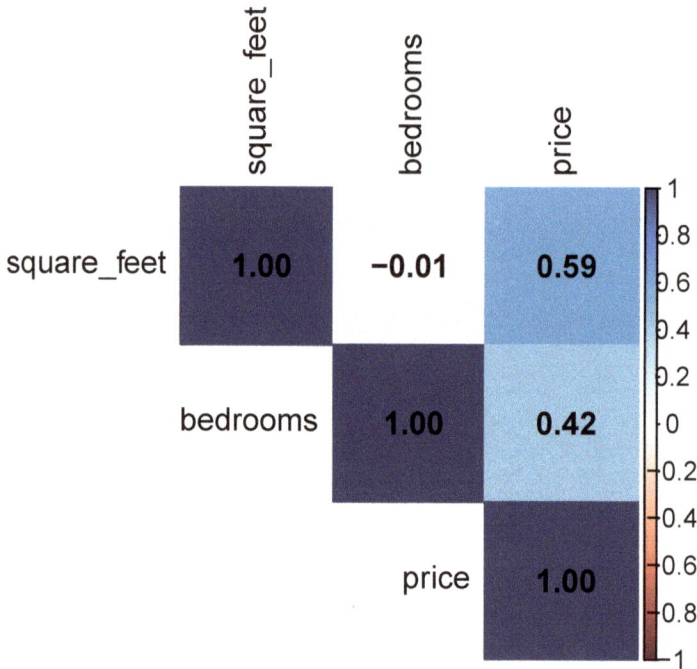

This heatmap-like chart gives you a quick overview of potential feature re-dundancy. By filtering out features that are highly correlated with each other, we reduce model complexity and can often achieve better general-ization performance on new, unseen data.

Step 6: Correlation Is Not Causation

A spurious correlation is a statistical relationship between two variables that appears meaningful, but is misleading and does not reflect a causal connec-tion. Instead, both variables are influenced by a third factor—often called a confounder—that creates the illusion of a relationship between them.

Let's demonstrate this classic principle using a simulated example: a strong positive correlation between ice cream sales and sunburn cases. At first glance, it may seem like eating more ice cream causes more sunburn. But that interpretation doesn't make sense—these two events are linked not by cause and effect, but by a common cause: hot summer weather.

This is a key reason why correlation does not imply causation. Just because two things move together statistically doesn't mean one is responsible for the other. If we mistakenly assume a causal relationship from correlation alone, we risk drawing incorrect or even harmful conclusions.

We'll now simulate this scenario in R and use it to explore a real-looking, but ultimately meaningless, correlation:

R Code
```
summer_data <- data.frame(
  month = 1:12,
  ice_cream_sales = c(100,120,150,200,250,300,
                      320,310,280,220,180,130),
  sunburn_cases = c(20,25,35,60,90,100,110,105,80,50,30,25)
)

# Correlation between unrelated variables
cor(summer_data$ice_cream_sales, summer_data$sunburn_cases)
```

Output
```
## [1] 0.9667585
```

R Code
```
# Plot
ggplot(summer_data, aes(x = ice_cream_sales,
                        y = sunburn_cases)) +
  geom_point(color = "#323232") +
  geom_smooth(method = "lm", se = FALSE, color = "#EE6C4D") +
  labs(title = "Spurious Correlation: Ice Cream vs. Sunburn",
       x = "Ice Cream Sales", y = "Sunburn Cases")
```

Spurious Correlation: Ice Cream vs. Sunburn

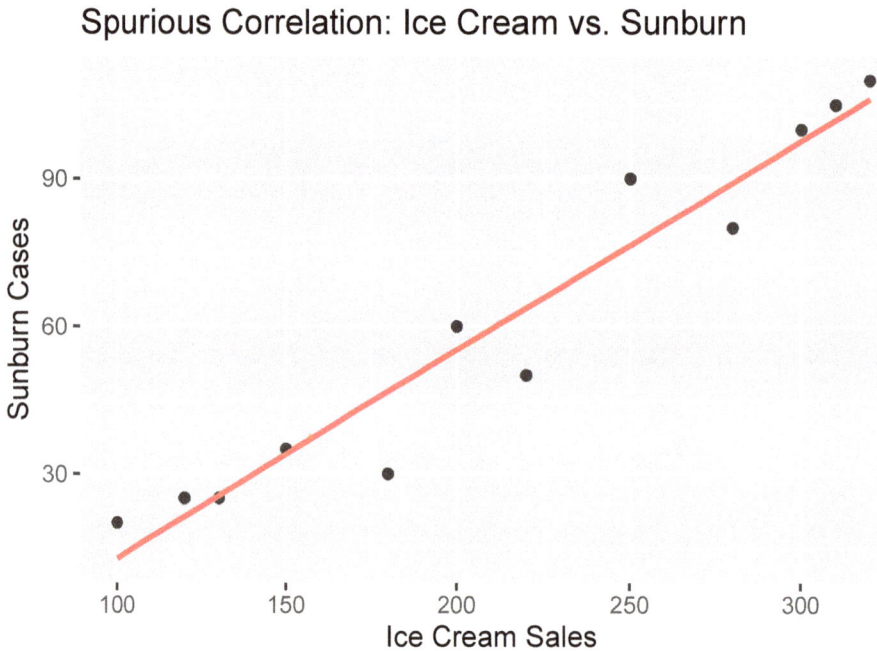

A correlation of around 0.97 might look impressive—but it doesn't mean eating more ice cream causes more sunburns. Both are influenced by summer weather, a hidden third variable.

Step 7: Causal Inference (Simplified)

In data analysis, it's not enough to just spot relationships—we often want to go deeper and ask: Did one thing cause another? This question is the heart of causal inference, a field that goes beyond correlation to determine whether a change in one variable causes a change in another.

For example, imagine a company runs a marketing campaign and sees a rise in sales. That's a correlation—but how do we know the campaign caused the increase? Maybe sales have risen due to other factors like seasonality or competitor issues. To test causation, we need to use a method that mimics a scientific experiment.

One reliable approach is to randomly assign people to two groups: one group sees the campaign (treatment group) and the other does not (control group). If the treatment group has significantly higher sales than the control group, and the only difference is who saw the campaign, we have good reason to infer causality.

Let's simulate this kind of experiment using randomly generated data in R:

```
R Code
set.seed(42)
n <- 100
group <- sample(c("Campaign", "No Campaign"), n,
              replace = TRUE)
sales <- ifelse(group == "Campaign", rnorm(n, 150, 10),
              rnorm(n, 130, 10))
campaign_data <- data.frame(group, sales)

# Compare means
tapply(campaign_data$sales, campaign_data$group, mean)
```

Output

```
##      Campaign No Campaign
##      149.3815    129.5693
```

R Code

```
# Visualize
ggplot(campaign_data, aes(x = group, y = sales,
                      fill = group)) +
  geom_boxplot() +
  labs(title = "Causal Inference: Campaign vs. No Campaign",
       y = "Sales")+
  scale_fill_manual(values = c("Campaign" = "#EE6C4D",
                            "No Campaign" = "#637D8D"))
```

Causal Inference: Campaign vs. No Campaign

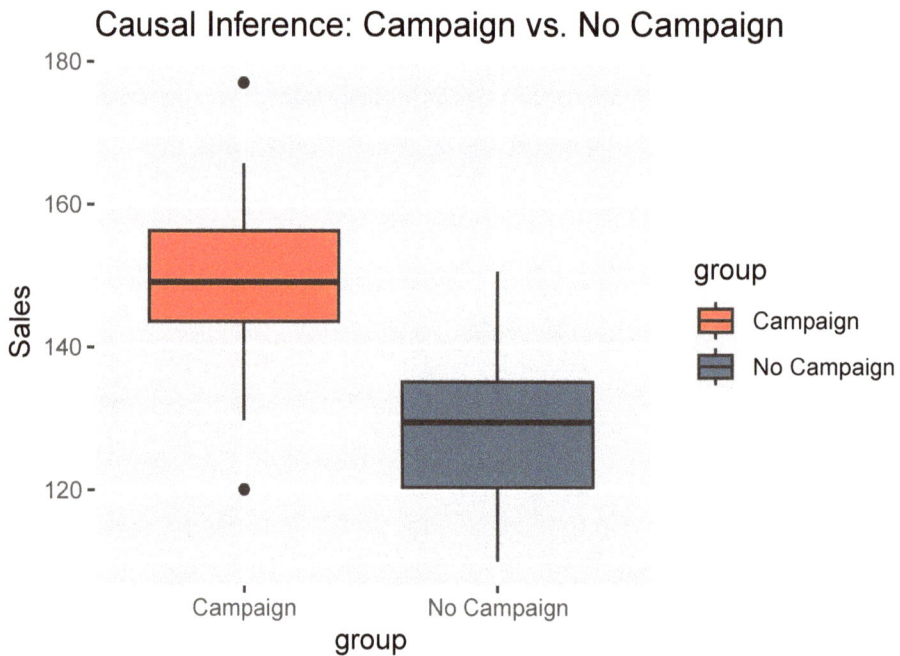

Since group assignments were random, any observed difference in outcomes—such as higher sales in the campaign group—can be interpreted as a causal effect of the campaign. This is because randomization ensures that, on average, all other factors that could influence sales (like customer preferences, income, geography, time of day, etc.) are evenly distributed between the two groups.

In other words, the only systematic difference between the two groups is exposure to the campaign. So, if we see that the campaign group has significantly higher sales, we can reasonably conclude that the campaign caused the increase.

This is what makes randomized experiments (like A/B tests) the gold standard for causal inference. They eliminate many sources of bias and confounding that can plague observational data, where group membership isn't controlled.

In contrast, if we had just looked at customers who chose to view the campaign (rather than assigning them randomly), it would be hard to tell whether sales were higher because of the campaign or because people who were already likely to buy happened to see it. That's the danger of self-selection bias—and randomization helps protect us against it.

Wrap-Up

In this lab, you learned how to use both Pearson and Spearman correlation methods to assess relationships between variables, each suited to different types of data and patterns. You also practiced visualizing these correlations through scatterplots and regression lines, which help reveal the strength and nature of the relationships. Additionally, you explored the critical distinction between correlation and causation, understanding that a strong correlation does not necessarily mean one variable causes the other..

Exercises

Correlation and Causality

Dataset 1: Car Performance Data

```
R Code
set.seed(10)
car_data <- data.frame(
  horsepower = rnorm(100, mean = 150, sd = 30),
  weight = rnorm(100, mean = 3000, sd = 500),
  mpg = rnorm(100, mean = 25, sd = 5)
)
```

1. Calculate the Pearson correlation between `horsepower` and `mpg`.
2. Calculate the Pearson correlation between `weight` and `mpg`.
3. Create a scatterplot with a regression line for `horsepower` vs. `mpg`.
4. Calculate the Spearman correlation between `weight` and `mpg`.
5. Create a scatterplot for `weight` vs. `mpg` and describe the relationship pattern.

Dataset 2: Student Exam Data

```
R Code
set.seed(42)
student_data <- data.frame(
  hours_studied = rnorm(80, mean = 5, sd = 2),
  attendance = round(runif(80, min = 60, max = 100)),
  exam_score = rnorm(80, mean = 75, sd = 10)
)
```

6. Compute the Pearson correlation matrix for all numeric variables.
7. Visualize the correlation matrix using `corrplot`.
8. Identify which variables have the strongest correlation with `exam_score`.
9. Discuss the implications of having strongly correlated predictors when building a predictive model.
10. How does the visualization help in interpreting relationships?

Dataset 3: Ice Cream and Colds

```
R Code
ice_cream_data <- data.frame(
  day = 1:30,
  ice_cream_sales = c(80, 90, 95, 110, 120, 130, 135, 140,
                      130, 125,120, 115, 100, 90, 80, 70,
                      65, 60, 55, 50, 45, 40, 35, 30, 25,
                      20, 15, 10, 5, 0),
  cold_symptoms_cases = c(15, 14, 14, 13, 12, 12, 11,
                      11, 10, 9,
                      9, 8, 8, 7, 7, 6, 6, 6, 5, 5,
                      4, 4, 4, 3, 3, 3, 2, 2, 1, 1)
)
```

11. Calculate the correlation between ice_cream_sales and cold_symptoms_cases in ice_cream_data.
12. Create a scatterplot with regression line for ice_cream_sales vs cold_symptoms_cases.
13. Explain why these two variables might be correlated but not causally related.

Lab 9

Sampling and Sampling Distributions

Sampling and sampling distributions are fundamental in statistics. When we select random samples, we aim to capture the characteristics of the entire population fairly and without bias. However, if samples are biased (not random) our analyses can become misleading. To address variability and estimate the reliability of our statistics, techniques like bootstrapping resample the data repeatedly with replacement, creating many pseudo-samples.

Lesson Steps

Step 1: Install & Load Required Package

We'll use the Tidyverse package for data manipulation and sampling.

```
R Code
options(repos = c(CRAN = "https://cran.r-project.org"))
install.packages("tidyverse")
library(tidyverse)
```

Step 2: Random Sampling

Random sampling is a technique used to select a subset of data that fairly represents the full dataset. In random sampling every member of the population has an equal chance of selection in the sample. By randomly selecting samples, we minimize bias and capture the diversity of the population.

Here, we randomly sample 10 cars from the built-in mtcars dataset.

```
R Code
data <- mtcars


set.seed(123)  # For reproducibility
sample_data <- sample_n(data, 10)


print(sample_data)
```

Output

```
##                     mpg cyl  disp  hp
## Maserati Bora       15.0   8 301.0 335
## Cadillac Fleetwood  10.4   8 472.0 205
## Honda Civic         30.4   4  75.7  52
## Merc 450SLC         15.2   8 275.8 180
## Datsun 710          22.8   4 108.0  93
## Merc 280            19.2   6 167.6 123
## Fiat 128            32.4   4  78.7  66
## Dodge Challenger    15.5   8 318.0 150
## Merc 280C           17.8   6 167.6 123
## Hornet Sportabout   18.7   8 360.0 175
##                     drat    wt  qsec vs
## Maserati Bora       3.54 3.570 14.60  0
## Cadillac Fleetwood  2.93 5.250 17.98  0
## Honda Civic         4.93 1.615 18.52  1
## Merc 450SLC         3.07 3.780 18.00  0
## Datsun 710          3.85 2.320 18.61  1
## Merc 280            3.92 3.440 18.30  1
## Fiat 128            4.08 2.200 19.47  1
## Dodge Challenger    2.76 3.520 16.87  0
## Merc 280C           3.92 3.440 18.90  1
## Hornet Sportabout   3.15 3.440 17.02  0
##                     am gear carb
## Maserati Bora        1    5    8
## Cadillac Fleetwood   0    3    4
## Honda Civic          1    4    2
## Merc 450SLC          0    3    3
## Datsun 710           1    4    1
## Merc 280             0    4    4
## Fiat 128             1    4    1
```

```
## Dodge Challenger     0    3    2
## Merc 280C            0    4    4
## Hornet Sportabout    0    3    2
```

The output shows a randomly selected group of 10 cars, each with attributes such as miles per gallon (mpg), horsepower, and weight. Because the seed is set, this sample can be reproduced exactly. Changing the sample size or seed will yield different samples.

Step 3: Biased Sampling

Let's sample only cars with mpg greater than 25 — a biased, non-diverse subset.

R Code
```
biased_sample <- subset(data, mpg > 25)
print(biased_sample)
```

Output

```
##                  mpg cyl  disp   hp drat
## Fiat 128        32.4   4  78.7   66 4.08
## Honda Civic     30.4   4  75.7   52 4.93
## Toyota Corolla  33.9   4  71.1   65 4.22
## Fiat X1-9       27.3   4  79.0   66 4.08
## Porsche 914-2   26.0   4 120.3   91 4.43
## Lotus Europa    30.4   4  95.1  113 3.77
##                   wt  qsec vs am gear
## Fiat 128        2.200 19.47  1  1    4
## Honda Civic     1.615 18.52  1  1    4
## Toyota Corolla  1.835 19.90  1  1    4
## Fiat X1-9       1.935 18.90  1  1    4
## Porsche 914-2   2.140 16.70  0  1    5
## Lotus Europa    1.513 16.90  1  1    5
##                 carb
## Fiat 128           1
## Honda Civic        2
## Toyota Corolla     1
## Fiat X1-9          1
## Porsche 914-2      2
## Lotus Europa       2
```

This subset includes only high-mpg cars and excludes many others, creating a biased dataset. Building models or drawing conclusions from such data is usually very misleading and just not good. (Unfortunately it is very common to use biased data).

Step 4: Bootstrapping Basics

Bootstrapping is a technique to replicate samples. Bootstrapping (a term of frugality) lets us stick with what we already have. Here's how it works: we create lots of new samples by randomly picking data points from the original dataset with replacement. This mimics the natural variation we might see if we had multiple datasets. Doing this allows us to estimate variability in the data. This helps us build confidence intervals and test hypothesis when it would not otherwise be possible.

Bootstrapping is especially useful in data science because real-world data isn't always perfect. It might not meet the requirements that traditional methods need, or we might just have a small dataset.

Now, let's create a bootstrap sample and compare its average miles per gallon (mpg) to the average mpg in the original dataset.

R Code
```
bootstrap_sample <- sample_n(mtcars, size = nrow(mtcars),
                             replace = TRUE)


mean_original <- mean(mtcars$mpg)
mean_bootstrap <- mean(bootstrap_sample$mpg)


cat("Original Mean MPG:", mean_original, "\n")
```

Output
```
## Original Mean MPG: 20.09062
```

R Code
```
cat("Bootstrap Mean MPG:", mean_bootstrap, "\n")
```

Output

```
## Bootstrap Mean MPG: 21.09375
```

Step 5: Repeating Bootstrapping and Visualizing Distribution

To better understand the variability, we repeat bootstrapping 1,000 times, collecting the mean mpg from each sample. This produces a distribution of mean values that reflects the uncertainty in our estimate.

R Code

```
bootstrap_means <- replicate(
  1000,
  mean(sample(mtcars$mpg, size = nrow(mtcars),
            replace = TRUE))
)

hist(bootstrap_means,
     main = "Bootstrap Distribution of Mean MPG",
     xlab = "Mean MPG", col = "#293241", border = "white")
```

Bootstrap Distribution of Mean MPG

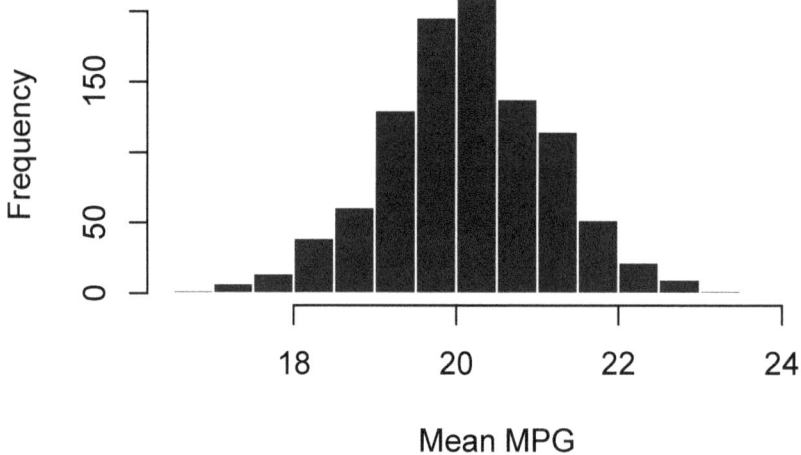

The histogram shows how these means vary, giving us insight into the natural variability of the average mpg.

Step 6: Estimating Confidence Intervals from Bootstrap Results

From the bootstrap distribution, we can estimate confidence intervals to express the range where the true mean mpg likely falls. For example, a 90% confidence interval means we are 90% confident that the population mean lies within this range.

R Code
```
quantile(bootstrap_means, probs = c(0.05, 0.95))
```

Output

```
##          5%        95%
## 18.37813 21.84703
```

This gives the 5th and 95th percentiles of the bootstrap means, forming a 90% confidence interval. Bootstrapping provides a straightforward way to assess uncertainty without relying on complex formulas, just by repeated resampling.

Wrap-Up

In this lab, you learned how to perform random sampling to obtain representative subsets of data that fairly reflect the characteristics of the whole population. Additionally, you explored the basics of bootstrapping, a powerful resampling technique used to estimate the variability of statistics by creating many pseudo-samples from the original data. Finally, you learned how to generate and interpret a bootstrap distribution and use it to calculate confidence intervals, which help quantify the uncertainty around your estimates.

Exercises

Sampling and Sampling Distributions

In this exercise you will practice random sampling, understand potential sampling biases, and apply bootstrapping to estimate variability and confidence intervals.

Dataset 1: Student Test Scores

```
R Code
set.seed(101)
student_scores <- data.frame(
  student_id = 1:50,
  math_score = round(rnorm(50, mean=75, sd=10)),
  reading_score = round(rnorm(50, mean=80, sd=8)),
  gender = sample(c("Male", "Female"), 50, replace = TRUE)
)
```

1. Use `sample_n()` to randomly select 8 students from `student_scores`. Display their data.
2. Calculate the mean math score for the full dataset and the sample from question 1.
3. Create a biased subset with only students who scored above 85 in reading. How many students are in this subset?
4. Using the original dataset, create a bootstrap sample with replacement of size 50 and calculate the mean math score of this bootstrap sample.
5. Repeat the bootstrap sampling 500 times, recording the mean math score each time. Plot a histogram of these bootstrap means.

Dataset 2: Customer Purchase Amounts

```
R Code
set.seed(202)
customer_purchases <- data.frame(
  customer_id = 1:100,
  purchase_amount = round(rexp(100, rate=0.05), 2),
  region = sample(c("North", "South", "East", "West"),
    100, replace = TRUE)
)
```

6. Take a random sample of 15 customers using `sample_n()`. Display their purchase amounts.

7. Calculate the average purchase amount for each region in the full dataset.

8. Create a biased subset with customers who spent more than $100. What is the average purchase amount in this subset?

9. Generate a bootstrap sample of size 100 with replacement from the original data and calculate the median purchase amount.

10. Repeat the bootstrap median calculation 1000 times and plot a histogram of these bootstrap medians. What does the distribution tell you about the median purchase amount?

Dataset 3: Daily Steps Recorded by Wearables

```
R Code
set.seed(303)
daily_steps <- data.frame(
  day = 1:60,
  steps = round(rnorm(60, mean=7000, sd=1500))
)
```

11. Select a random sample of 12 days and display the number of steps recorded.
12. Calculate the mean and standard deviation of steps in the full dataset.
13. Create a bootstrap sample of size 60 with replacement and calculate the mean steps in this sample.
14. Repeat bootstrapping 1000 times, recording the mean steps each time. Plot the bootstrap distribution of the mean steps.
15. Calculate a 95% confidence interval for the mean number of daily steps using the bootstrap distribution.

Lab 10

Regression and Predictive Modeling

Introduction

At its core, regression helps us understand how one or more variables are related to an outcome we care about. For example, you might want to know how a person's years of experience affect their salary, how the number of online ads influences sales, or what factors contribute to a customer's likelihood of buying a product.

By uncovering these relationships, regression allows us to make predictions based on data, which is incredibly useful in many fields. Whether you're estimating house prices, forecasting stock trends, or supporting decision-making in business or healthcare, regression turns raw data patterns into clear, actionable insights.

In this lab, we'll start with simple linear regression, which models the relationship between one predictor variable and a numeric outcome. Next, we'll explore logistic regression, a technique used for classification problems where the outcome is a category—such as yes/no or spam/not spam. Finally, we'll dive into multiple regression, which helps us analyze how several variables together influence an outcome.

Lesson Steps

Step 1: Load Your Tools

To get started, we load essential R packages for data manipulation and visualization. The `ggplot2` package provides flexible and clear plotting tools, while `dplyr` supports data manipulation. If you don't have these installed yet, you can install them once using `install.packages()`.

```
R Code
options(repos = c(CRAN = "https://cran.r-project.org"))
install.packages("ggplot2")
install.packages("dplyr")

library(ggplot2)
library(dplyr)
```

Step 2: Linear Regression

Linear regression is one of the simplest — and most useful — tools in data analysis. It helps us predict a number (like a salary or test score) based on one or more other factors (like experience or study time).

Think about this: as someone gains more years of work experience, their salary usually goes up. That's a relationship between two variables — and linear regression draws a straight line through data points to capture that relationship. The goal is to find the line that best fits the trend.

Let's create a data set.

R Code

```
experience <- c(1, 2, 3, 4, 5, 6, 7, 8)
salary <- c(32000, 34000, 36000, 39000, 41000, 43000,
            46000, 48000)
df <- data.frame(experience, salary)


model_linear <- lm(salary ~ experience, data = df)
summary(model_linear)
```

Output

```
##
## Call:
## lm(formula = salary ~ experience, data = df)
##
## Residuals:
##     Min      1Q  Median      3Q     Max
## -392.86 -142.86  -17.86  258.93  321.43
##
## Coefficients:
##             Estimate Std. Error t value
## (Intercept) 29428.57     232.83  126.40
## experience   2321.43      46.11   50.35
##             Pr(>|t|)
## (Intercept) 1.65e-11 ***
## experience  4.12e-09 ***
## ---
## Signif. codes:
##   0 '***' 0.001 '**' 0.01 '*' 0.05
##   '.' 0.1 ' ' 1
##
## Residual standard error: 298.8 on 6 degrees of freedom
## Multiple R-squared:  0.9976, Adjusted R-squared:  0.9972
## F-statistic:  2535 on 1 and 6 DF,  p-value: 4.118e-09
```

The model summary shows the intercept and slope. The intercept (around 29,429) estimates the salary at zero years of experience, while the slope (about 2,321) indicates that each additional year of experience increases salary by roughly $2,321. The regression equation can be written as:

Salary = 29,428.57 + 2,321.43 × experience

Let's visualize the data points along with the regression line.

```
R Code
ggplot(df, aes(x = experience, y = salary)) +
  geom_point(color = "#3D5A80") +
  geom_smooth(method = "lm", se = FALSE, color = "#98C1D9") +
  labs(title = "Linear Regression: Salary vs. Experience",
       x = "Years of Experience", y = "Salary")
```

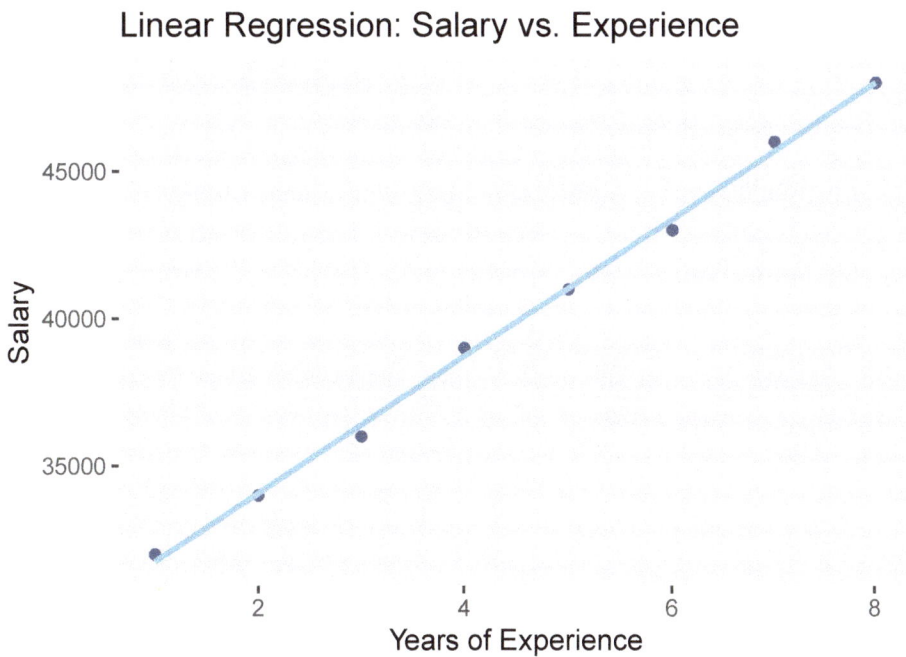

Linear Regression: Salary vs. Experience

The scatterplot shows a clear upward trend, with the regression line capturing the strong positive relationship between experience and salary.

Step 3: Logistic Regression

Sometimes in data analysis, we don't want to predict a number — we want to answer a yes-or-no question. That's where logistic regression comes in.

Instead of predicting things like height or salary (which are numeric), logistic regression helps us predict categories — for example, whether an email is spam or not spam, or whether a customer will buy something or not. These are called binary outcomes because there are just two options: 1 (yes) or 0 (no).

Here's how it works: the model looks at one or more input variables (like the number of links in an email) and estimates the probability that the outcome is a 1 (like "yes, it's spam"). It uses something called the logistic function to make sure that probability stays between 0 and 1.

Here is a simple example: a small dataset of emails labeled as spam or not. We'll focus on one predictor — the number of links in the email — and build a logistic regression model to see how that affects the chances of it being spam.

```
R Code
# Set R's output width
options(width = 30)


spam <- c(1, 0, 1, 0, 1, 0, 0, 1)
links <- c(10, 1, 8, 2, 9, 1, 2, 7)
df_spam <- data.frame(spam, links)


model_log <- glm(spam ~ links, data = df_spam,
                 family = "binomial")
coef(model_log)
```

Output
```
## (Intercept)        links
##  -43.510832     9.573618
```

The output shows coefficients for the intercept and the links variable. A positive coefficient suggests that emails with more links are more likely to be spam. However, the small sample size here results in large standard errors and non-significant p-values, so treat this as an illustrative example.

We can still use the model to predict the probability that a new email with 5 links is spam.

R Code
```
new_email <- data.frame(links = 5)
predict(model_log, new_email, type = "response")
```

Output
```
##              1
## 0.9873486
```

The model predicts a probability of about 98.7%, meaning it classifies the email as spam since the probability is greater than 0.5.

Step 4: Multiple Regression

Multiple regression is what we turn to when one variable just isn't enough to explain what's going on. In real-world data, outcomes are rarely driven by a single factor. Multiple regression builds on simple linear regression by allowing us to examine the effect of two or more predictors at the same time (note you can also have multiple logistic regression with more the one input something we will not do here). This gives us a more realistic understanding of how different variables work together to influence a result.

Imagine we're trying to predict the accuracy of a machine learning model. It wouldn't make sense to only look at the size of the dataset — accuracy could also depend on how many features the model is using, or how powerful the computer is (say, the number of GPU cores). Multiple regression lets us take all these variables into account at once. We can then figure out which ones have the strongest impact, and how they combine to affect the outcome.

First let's simulate a dataset.

R Code
```
# Set R's output width
options(width = 30)



dataset_size <- c(5000, 7000, 9000, 11000, 13000)
features <- c(25, 35, 45, 30, 50)
gpu_cores <- c(2, 5, 3, 7, 4)
accuracy <- c(66, 72, 74, 79, 81)


df_multi <- data.frame(dataset_size, features,
                 gpu_cores, accuracy)
model_multi <- lm(accuracy ~ dataset_size +
                features + gpu_cores,
                data = df_multi)
coef(model_multi)
```

```
Output
##   (Intercept) dataset_size
## 55.362428161   0.001451509
##      features     gpu_cores
##   0.071839080   0.789511494
```

The model coefficients show how accuracy changes with each predictor, holding others constant. For example, increasing dataset size by one unit increases accuracy by about 0.00145%, adding a feature increases accuracy by roughly 0.072%, and each additional GPU core raises accuracy by approximately 0.79%. The high R-squared indicates the model fits the data well, and p-values under 0.05 suggest these relationships are statistically significant.

Wrap-Up

This lab was about key regression techniques used for prediction and classification. Linear regression helps predict continuous outcomes and understand simple relationships. Logistic regression models probabilities for binary outcomes, essential for classification tasks. Multiple regression enables you to analyze how several variables jointly influence an outcome, offering more nuanced insights.

Exercises

Regression and Predictive Modeling

In these exercises you practice building and interpreting regression models in R, including simple linear regression, logistic regression, and multiple regression.

Dataset 1: Simple Linear Regression — Predicting House Prices

This dataset contains data on house size (in square feet) and house prices (in $1000s).

```
R Code
# Dataset 1
set.seed(100)
house_size <- c(850, 900, 1200, 1500, 1700, 1900, 2200, 2500)
house_price <- c(150, 160, 200, 230, 250, 270, 310, 350)
df_house <- data.frame(house_size, house_price)
```

1. Fit a simple linear regression model to predict house price using house size.
2. What are the intercept and slope coefficients of your model?
3. Write out the regression equation based on your model coefficients.
4. Using your model, predict the price of a house that is 2000 sq ft.
5. Create a scatter plot of house_size vs. house_price with the regression line overlaid.

Dataset 2: Logistic Regression — Predicting Loan Default

This dataset contains information about whether a borrower defaulted on a loan (1 = default, 0 = no default) and their credit score.

```
R Code
# Dataset 2
loan_default <- c(0, 0, 1, 0, 1, 1, 0, 1, 0, 1)
credit_score <- c(700, 720, 680, 710, 650, 630, 690,
                  640, 720, 660)
df_loan <- data.frame(loan_default, credit_score)
```

6. Fit a logistic regression model to predict loan_default using credit_score.
7. What is the sign of the credit_score coefficient, and what does it imply about credit score and default risk?
8. Calculate the predicted probability of default for a borrower with a credit score of 670.
9. Calculate the predicted probability of default for a borrower with a credit score of 710.
10. Plot the predicted probabilities of default against credit scores along with the observed data points.

Dataset 3: Multiple Regression — Predicting Car Fuel Efficiency

This dataset has variables for car weight (in 1000 lbs), engine horsepower, and fuel efficiency (mpg).

```
R Code
# Dataset 3
car_weight <- c(2.2, 2.5, 3.0, 3.2, 3.5, 3.8, 4.0, 4.2)
horsepower <- c(130, 150, 165, 180, 200, 210, 220, 230)
mpg <- c(33, 30, 28, 25, 23, 22, 20, 18)
df_car <- data.frame(car_weight, horsepower, mpg)
```

11. Fit a multiple linear regression model to predict mpg using car_weight and horsepower as predictors.
12. Report the estimated regression coefficients for car_weight and horsepower.
13. Interpret the coefficient for car_weight in your model.
14. Use your model to predict the mpg for a car weighing 3.3 (1000 lbs) with 170 horsepower.
15. Create visualizations (either a 3D scatter plot or multiple 2D plots) to illustrate the relationship between mpg, car_weight, and horsepower.

Lab 11

Hypothesis Testing and P-Values

When we compare two groups — like two different machine learning models or two marketing campaigns — and notice a difference, the big question is: Is that difference real, or just random noise? Hypothesis testing is the formal statistical technique to answer this.

The process starts with two competing ideas. The null hypothesis assumes there's no real difference — that any variation we see is just by chance. The alternative hypothesis, on the other hand, says there is a real effect — that one model truly performs better, or one campaign really does work more effectively than the other.

Once we have these hypotheses, we compare our data to what we'd expect if the null hypothesis were true. This leads us to a key number: the p-value. The smaller the p-value, the less likely our results happened by chance. If it's small enough, we have evidence to reject the null and lean toward the alternative — in other words, we have reason to believe the difference is real.

There are numerous variaties of hypothesis test but one of the most comm-mon is to compare two groups what we will explore here.

Lesson Steps

Step 1: Make Data

Let's generate example test scores to compare the performance of two predictive models. Model A represents the current standard, with scores ranging mostly in the high 70s to low 80s, while Model B is a new model showing higher scores mostly in the mid to high 80s. These sample scores allow us to analyze whether Model B truly performs better than Model A or if the difference could be due to chance.

```
R Code
model_a_scores <- c(80, 82, 78, 76, 79, 81, 77, 80, 83, 78)
model_b_scores <- c(85, 88, 84, 86, 87, 89, 84, 88, 90, 85)
```

Step 2: Define Hypotheses

Now we set up our hypotheses. These are formal statements that frame the question we're asking:

- **Null Hypothesis:** Model A and Model B have the same average score.

- **Alternative Hypothesis:** Model A and Model B have different average scores.

This is called a two-sided test (or two-tailed test) because we're not assuming in advance which model is better. We're simply asking: Is there any difference at all between the two models' average scores.

Step 3: Run a t-test

To test whether there is any difference between the average scores of Model A and Model B, we use a two-sided t-test. This test checks if the means are different in either direction.

```
R Code
# Set R's output width
options(width = 30)


t.test(model_b_scores, model_a_scores,
        alternative = "two.sided")
```

This command compares the two sets of scores and calculates whether the observed difference in means is statistically significant, without assuming which model is better.

Step 4: Interpret the Output

After running the t-test, you'll see output like this (your exact numbers may vary slightly):

```
        Welch Two Sample t-test

data:  model_b_scores and model_a_scores
t = 7.4175, df = 17.96, p-value = 7.168e-07
alternative hypothesis: true difference
  in means is not equal to 0
95 percent confidence interval:
 5.160349 9.239651
sample estimates:
mean of x mean of y
     86.6      79.4
```

Let's interpret the t-test output in more detail. The t-value of 7.42 indicates that the difference between the two models' average scores is large compared to the variation within the samples. The degrees of freedom, which account for sample size and variance, help determine the exact distribution to compare this t-value against. Most importantly, the p-value is extremely small (7.168e-07), providing strong evidence that the difference we observe is unlikely to be due to random chance alone. The confidence interval shows that the true difference in average scores between Model B and Model A is likely between 5.2 and 9.2 points, clearly favoring Model B. Finally, the sample means reveal that Model B has an average score of 86.6, while Model A's average is 79.4, confirming that Model B performs better in this example.

Step 5: Understand the p-value

The p-value helps us understand how likely it is to see a difference as large as the one in our data—or even larger—if the null hypothesis were true, meaning if there really was no difference between the models. A small p-value, typically less than 0.05, indicates that such a large difference would be very unlikely to happen by chance alone. In our example, the p-value is extremely small and far below the 0.05 threshold. Because of this, we reject the null hypothesis and conclude that there is evidence to concolude that Model A and Model B have different average scores.

Wrap-up

This lab demonstrated how hypothesis testing helps us decide whether a difference between two groups is real or just due to chance. Using a two-sided t-test, we compared the average scores of two models and found strong evidence that Model B outperforms Model A. The process—setting up hypotheses, running the test, interpreting the p-value, and drawing a conclusion—is the core of how hypothesis testing works.

While we used a t-test here, the same logic applies across many situations. For proportions, you'd use a proportion test; for more than two groups, ANOVA; for categorical data, a chi-squared test; and for paired comparisons, a paired t-test or McNemar's test. Regardless of the type, all hypothesis tests follow the same basic steps.

Exercises

Hypothesis Testing and P-Values

In this exercise, you'll practice comparing two independent groups using two-sample t-tests.

Dataset 1: Comparing Test Scores Between Two Teaching Methods

Students are taught using two different methods. You want to see if there's a significant difference in their average scores.

```
R Code
# Dataset 1
method_a <- c(75, 78, 74, 72, 70, 77, 76, 74, 73, 75)
method_b <- c(80, 82, 79, 81, 83, 78, 80, 82, 79, 81)

df_scores <- data.frame(
  method = rep(c("A", "B"), each = 10),
  score = c(method_a, method_b)
)
```

1. What is the mean score for each teaching method?
2. Write the null and alternative hypotheses for comparing the two methods.
3. Use t.test() to compare the scores. Paste your code and output.
4. What does the p-value tell you? Can you reject the null hypothesis?
5. Create a boxplot comparing scores between the two methods.

Dataset 2: Comparing Daily Step Counts by Gender

This is hypothetical data comparing daily step counts between two independent groups: men and women.

```
R Code
# Dataset 2
men_steps <- c(7200, 6800, 7000, 7500, 7300, 6900,
              7100, 7400, 7200, 7000)
women_steps <- c(8100, 8300, 8000, 7900, 8200,
                8050, 8150, 8000, 8100, 8250)

df_steps <- data.frame(
  gender = rep(c("Men", "Women"), each = 10),
  steps = c(men_steps, women_steps)
)
```

6. What are the mean step counts for men and women?
7. What are the null and alternative hypotheses for this comparison?
8. Use a two-sample t-test to test for a significant difference in step counts.
9. Interpret the p-value in context. Does one group appear to walk more on average?
10. Create a boxplot comparing daily step counts by gender.

Dataset 3 Comparing Hours of Sleep for Early vs. Late Chronotypes

```
R Code
# Dataset 3
early_sleep <- c(7.5, 8, 7, 7.2, 7.8, 8.1,
                 7.6, 7.9, 8.2, 7.3)
late_sleep <- c(6.8, 6.5, 6.9, 6.6, 6.4, 6.7,
                 6.5, 6.3, 6.6, 6.2)

df_sleep <- data.frame(
  type = rep(c("Early", "Late"), each = 10),
  hours = c(early_sleep, late_sleep)
)
```

11. Find the mean sleep duration for early vs. late chronotypes.
12. Run a t-test and determine if the difference is statistically significant.
13. Make a plot to visualize the difference in average hours of sleep.

Lab 12

Data Cleaning Techniques

Data cleaning is a crucial step in any data analysis workflow and should usually be done before any further analysis. Common things that need cleaning include data may contain missing values, duplicates, outliers, and inconsistent formats that can lead to incorrect conclusions if not addressed.

In this lab, you will learn some basic data cleaning techniques. These include handling missing data, removing duplicates, identifying outliers, and standardizing data formats.

Lesson Steps

Step 1: Setup

We start by loading the tidyverse, which includes tools like dplyr, tidyr, readr, and ggplot2—all built to work smoothly together.

```
R Code
options(repos = c(CRAN = "https://cran.r-project.org"))
# Install packages (run once if needed)
install.packages("tidyverse")


# Load libraries
library(tidyverse)
```

Step 2: Handling Missing Data

Missing data is one of the messy parts of working with real datasets— it is annoying and confusing to deal with. How you handle it can make or break your analysis. Two of the most common ways to fix it are imputation and removal.

Imputation means filling in the blanks with your best guess. For instance, if some Age values are missing, you might replace them with the average age from the rest of the dataset. It's a practical way to keep as much data as possible without making wild assumptions.

Removal, on the other hand, means cutting rows entirely—especially when key information, like Salary, is missing and can't be estimated reliably.

```
R Code
# Sample data with missing values
employees <- tibble(
  Name = c("Alice", "Bob", "Charlie", "Dana"),
  Age = c(25, NA, 30, NA),
  Salary = c(50000, 60000, NA, 55000)
)


print(employees)
```

Output
```
## # A tibble: 4 x 3
##    Name        Age Salary
##    <chr>     <dbl>  <dbl>
## 1 Alice        25  50000
## 2 Bob          NA  60000
## 3 Charlie      30     NA
## 4 Dana         NA  55000
```

R Code
```
# Impute missing Age with mean age
mean_age <- mean(employees$Age, na.rm = TRUE)
employees$Age[is.na(employees$Age)] <- mean_age

# Remove rows where Salary is missing
employees_clean <- employees[!is.na(employees$Salary), ]
print(employees_clean)
```

Output
```
## # A tibble: 3 x 3
##    Name     Age Salary
##    <chr> <dbl>  <dbl>
## 1 Alice    25   50000
## 2 Bob    27.5   60000
## 3 Dana   27.5   55000
```

After filling in the missing Age values with the average age, and removing rows where Salary is missing, the dataset no longer has any gaps of missing data.

Step 3: Dealing with Duplicates

Duplicate records sneak into datasets for all sorts of reasons — maybe a typo during data entry, combining files without double-checking, or glitches in the system. But these repeats can mess up your analysis by making some data points count more than they should. Imagine a customer showing up multiple times — suddenly your totals and averages get thrown off.

Dealing with duplicates means scanning your data for rows that look the same in important columns and deleting the extras.

```
R Code
# Sample data with duplicates
orders <- tibble(
  OrderID = c(101, 102, 102, 103),
  Customer = c("A", "B", "B", "C")
)

# Remove duplicate rows
orders_unique <- distinct(orders)
print(orders_unique)
```

```
Output
## # A tibble: 3 x 2
##    OrderID Customer
##      <dbl> <chr>
## 1      101 A
## 2      102 B
## 3      103 C
```

In this example, we start with a small dataset called orders that contains four records. Each record has an OrderID and a corresponding Customer. Notice that the order with OrderID 102 and customer "B" appears twice, meaning there is a duplicate row.

To clean the dataset, we use the distinct() function from the dplyr package, which removes duplicate rows by keeping only unique combinations of all columns. When we apply distinct() to the orders data, it removes the repeated entry for order 102 and customer "B," resulting in a smaller dataset with only unique rows.

The printed output orders_unique shows three rows, each representing a distinct order and customer pair.

Step 4: Identifying Outliers

Outliers are data points that are unusually large or small compared to the rest of the values in a dataset. These extreme values can arise for various reasons, such as measurement errors, data entry mistakes, or naturally rare but valid occurrences. Outliers are important to identify because they can significantly distort statistical analyses, skew summary statistics like means and standard deviations, and affect the performance of machine learning models.

Outliers can be detected by visualizing the data using boxplots. A boxplot provides a graphical summary of the distribution, highlighting the median, quartiles, and potential outliers. Points that fall far outside the typical range of the data appear as individual dots beyond the "whiskers" of the boxplot, making them easy to spot.

Outliers can also be detected using the Interquartile Range (IQR) rule. The IQR is the range between the first quartile (25th percentile) and the third quartile (75th percentile) of the data. Values that lie below the lower bound (Q1 - 1.5 × IQR) or above the upper bound (Q3 + 1.5 × IQR) are considered outliers.

However, it's important to carefully consider the context of outliers before removing them. Some outliers may represent valid extreme cases or important phenomena, so instead of automatic removal, they may require special attention or alternative modeling approaches.

In this example, we create dataset sales, which contains daily sales amounts over seven days. Most values fall between 200 and 230, but one value—1000 on day 5—stands out as much higher than the rest. This unusually large number is a classic example of an outlier.

```
R Code
# Sample data with an outlier
sales <- tibble(
  Day = 1:7,
  Amount = c(200, 220, 210, 215, 1000, 230, 225)
)


# Visualize sales with a boxplot
boxplot(sales$Amount, main = "Boxplot of Sales")
```

Boxplot of Sales

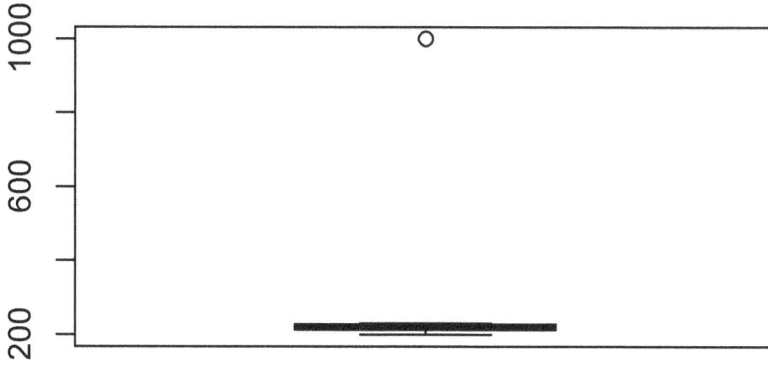

R Code

```
# Calculate IQR bounds
Q1 <- quantile(sales$Amount, 0.25)
Q3 <- quantile(sales$Amount, 0.75)
IQR_value <- Q3 - Q1


lower_bound <- Q1 - 1.5 * IQR_value
upper_bound <- Q3 + 1.5 * IQR_value


# Remove outliers
sales_clean <- filter(sales,
      Amount >= lower_bound & Amount <= upper_bound)


# Boxplot after outlier removal
boxplot(sales_clean$Amount,
      main = "Boxplot of Sales with Outlier Removed")
```

Boxplot of Sales with Outlier Removed

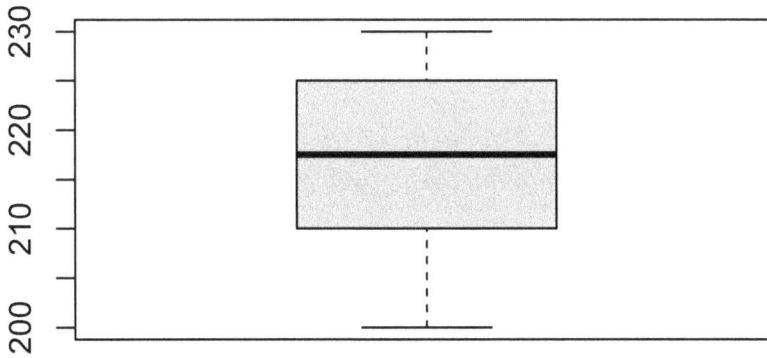

To visualize the distribution, we start by creating a boxplot. The plot clearly highlights the 1000 value as a point far above the rest of the data, confirming that it's an extreme outlier.

Next, we calculate the Interquartile Range (IQR), which measures the spread of the middle 50% of the data. We find the first quartile (Q1) and third quartile (Q3), then compute the IQR as Q3 - Q1. From there, we calculate cutoff values: anything below Q1 - 1.5 × IQR or above Q3 + 1.5 × IQR is flagged as an outlier.

Applying this rule to our data, we identify and remove the outlier value of 1000. We then generate a second boxplot with the cleaned dataset.

Step 5: Standardizing Formats

Maintaining consistent data formats across all variables is essential for accurate analysis. Different data sources often store information in varying formats, which can lead to errors or misinterpretation if not standardized before analysis. This issue goes beyond dates to include numeric values, categorical variables, text encoding, and more but is particularily rampant with date time data since different systms have different ways of entering these values.

For example, dates can appear in many different formats such as "YYYY-MM-DD", "MM/DD/YYYY", "DD-Mon-YYYY", or even timestamps with times included. Numeric data might use different decimal separators (". " vs ","), and categorical variables might have inconsistent capitalization (Ms., MS., Ms) or spelling. Without standardizing these formats, simple operations like filtering, grouping, or merging datasets can fail or produce incorrect results.

To handle these challenges, it is important to apply a consistent representation recognized by your analysis software for the format of data. Specifically for dates, the lubridate package part of the Tidyverse packages is useful. It provides intuitive functions to parse a wide variety of date and time formats and convert them into a standard R Date or POSIXct object. This consistency allows you to perform date arithmetic, comparisons, and visualizations reliably.

Before using lubridate, you need to install and load it:

```
R Code
options(repos = c(CRAN = "https://cran.r-project.org"))
# Install packages (run once if needed)
install.packages("lubridate")
library(lubridate)
```

In the example code, we start with a small dataset called dates that contains a column RawDate with dates in three different formats. To standardize the dates, the parse_date_time() function from lubridate is used.

```
R Code
# Example of messy dates
dates <- tibble(
  RawDate = c("01/05/2023", "2023-01-06", "05-Jan-2023")
)


# Convert to consistent date format
dates$CleanDate <- lubridate::parse_date_time(dates$RawDate,
                  orders = c("dmy", "ymd", "d-b-Y"))
print(dates)
```

```
Output
## # A tibble: 3 x 2
##    RawDate   CleanDate
##    <chr>     <dttm>
## 1 01/05/2~ 2023-05-01 00:00:00
## 2 2023-01~ 2023-01-06 00:00:00
## 3 05-Jan-~ 2023-01-05 00:00:00
```

After this conversion, a new column CleanDate is added to the dataset containing all dates in the same, standardized format. When printed, the resulting tibble shows the original messy RawDate alongside the cleaned and consistent CleanDate.

Wrap-Up

In this lab, you practiced essential data cleaning techniques. First, you learned how to handle missing data by imputing missing values with the mean and removing rows where critical information was missing. Next, you identified and removed duplicate records to ensure each data entry was unique, preventing biased results. You also explored detecting outliers using boxplots and the interquartile range method to filter extreme values that could distort analysis. Finally, you standardized inconsistent date formats using the lubridate package, making date data consistent and easy to work with.

Exercises

Data Cleaning Techniques

This exercise is for hands-on practice with basic data cleaning techniques. You'll handle missing values, remove duplicates, detect outliers, and standardize dates.

Dataset 1: Customers (Missing Data and Duplicate Removal)

```
R Code
library(tidyverse)

customers <- tibble(
  CustomerID = c(1, 2, 3, 4, 4, 5),
  Name = c("Alice", "Bob", "Carol", "David",
           "David", "Eve"),
  Age = c(28, NA, 35, 40, 40, NA),
  Spending = c(200, 150, NA, 250, 250, 300)
)
```

1. What is the mean age (excluding missing values)? Replace the missing Age values with this mean. Paste the updated dataset.
2. Remove rows where Spending is missing. How many rows remain? Paste the cleaned dataset.
3. Remove duplicate rows. Paste the deduplicated dataset.
4. What might go wrong if we keep rows with missing Spending?
5. Why does it matter to remove duplicates before analyzing customer behavior?

Dataset 2: Product Sales (Outlier Detection)

```
R Code
sales <- tibble(
  Product = LETTERS[1:10],
  UnitsSold = c(100, 120, 130, 110, 105, 300,
                115, 118, 108, 112)
)
```

6. Create a boxplot of UnitsSold. Paste the plot.
7. Calculate the IQR and find the lower and upper bounds. Paste the bounds.
8. Remove the outlier(s) based on the bounds. Paste the filtered dataset.
9. Create a boxplot of UnitsSold after removing outliers. Paste the plot.
10. Give one reason you might keep an outlier in your analysis.

Dataset 3: Orders with Inconsistent Dates (Date Format Cleaning)

```
R Code
library(lubridate)

orders <- tibble(
  OrderID = 1:5,
  RawDate = c("01-04-2024", "2024/01/05", "April 6, 2024",
              "2024.04.07", "06-Apr-2024")
)
```

11. Use parse_date_time() to standardize the dates. Paste the updated tibble.

12. What date formats did you include in the orders argument?
13. Give one reason why inconsistent date formats cause problems in analysis.

Lab 13

Data Importing and Exporting

Information can come in many forms—whether stored as simple CSV files, complex Excel spreadsheets with multiple sheets and formulas, structured JSON documents used in web applications or housed inside relational databases that organize data across multiple tables. Being able to efficiently import, export, and connect to these different data formats is a critical skill for any data analyst or scientist.

In this lab, you will focus on practical skills to manage your data files. You will learn how to set and manage file paths and working directories, which are essential for organizing your projects and ensuring your code can find and save files correctly. You will also practice importing data from and exporting data to CSV and Excel files. Finally, you will get an introductory overview of how to connect to relational databases.

Lesson Steps

Step 1: File Paths and Working Directory

When working with files in R, it's important to know where your files are being read from or saved to. This location is called the working directory. By default, R uses a specific folder as its working directory, but you can check

or change this to point to your project folder where your data and scripts
are stored. Managing the working directory correctly helps your code find
files without needing to write long paths each time, making your workflow
more organized and your scripts easier to share.

To check your current working directory, use getwd().

R Code
```
# Check the current working directory
getwd()
```

Note your result will be different as this is the writer's working directory
not yours. To change the working directory, use setwd() with the path to
your desired folder. Paths in R should use forward slashes / to work well
across different operating systems like Windows, Mac, or Linux. This can
also be done with pulldown menus if using RStudio (but cannot if on a non
IDE environment if using command line R).

R Code
```
# Set working directory  (Windows)
setwd("C:/Users/YourName/Documents/DataProjects/Project1")

# Set working directory (Mac/Linux)
setwd("/Users/YourName/Documents/DataProjects/Project1")
```

Instead of changing the working directory, you can also use absolute file
paths when reading or writing files. Absolute paths specify the full location
of the file, so you don't need to set the working directory first. Note the
direction of slashes in these.

Using absolute paths can be less flexible if you share your code with others
or run it on different computers, but they are useful when working with files

outside your current working directory.

Step 2: CSV Files

CSV (Comma-Separated Values) files are simple plain-text files that store tabular data, where each line represents a row and each value within that row is separated by a comma. Because of their straightforward structure, CSV files are easy to create, read, and edit using a wide range of software—from text editors to spreadsheet programs like Excel. This simplicity and compatibility make CSV one of the most common and widely used data formats for sharing data between different systems and tools. Whether you are exporting data from a database, receiving data from a colleague, or preparing data for analysis, CSV files offer a flexible and accessible way to organize and exchange tabular information.

Below, we create a simple data frame of employee information, save it as a CSV file, and then read it back into R. It will do this in the assigned working directory.

R Code

```r
# Create a simple data frame
employees <- data.frame(
  id = 1:3,
  name = c("Alice", "Bob", "Carol"),
  department = c("Sales", "HR", "IT")
)


# Write the data frame to a CSV file
write.csv(employees, "employees.csv", row.names = FALSE)


# Read the CSV file back into R
data_csv <- read.csv("employees.csv")


# Display the first few rows to verify
head(data_csv)
```

Output

```
##   id  name department
## 1  1 Alice      Sales
## 2  2   Bob         HR
## 3  3 Carol         IT
```

If successful, you will see the contents of the `employees.csv` file loaded correctly into R.

Step 3: Excel Files

Excel spreadsheets are one of the most popular tools for storing and sharing data in business and many other fields. Unlike simple CSV files, Excel files can contain multiple sheets, formatted cells, formulas, and other features that make them versatile for complex data management.

When working in R, you often need to import data from Excel files or export your analysis results back to Excel to share with others. R provides several packages to handle Excel files efficiently. Base R does NOT handle excel files so you do need to install a package..

The readxl package is widely used for reading Excel files because it is fast, simple, and does not require external dependencies. To read data from Excel, the read_excel() function from the readxl package imports data from an existing Excel file, for example "data.xlsx". You can specify the sheet to read by name or index, such as "Sheet1". The imported data is stored in a variable (here, excel_data) as a data frame that you can use for further analysis in R (note that you import only one sheet at a time when storing it int a data frame).

For writing Excel files, packages like writexl and openxlsx are popular choices. The writexl package is lightweight and easy to use for creating new Excel files. The write_xlsx() function from the writexl package writes a data frame—such as an example employees dataset—to a new Excel file named "employees_output.xlsx". This results in a simple Excel file with one sheet containing your data.

R Code
```
options(repos = c(CRAN = "https://cran.r-project.org"))
# Install packages if not already installed
install.packages("readxl")
install.packages("writexl")


# Load libraries
library(readxl)
library(writexl)
```

R Code
```
# Write a data frame to a new Excel file
# Note this data was produced in step 2
write_xlsx(employees, "employees_output.xlsx")


# Read data from a specific sheet in an Excel file
excel_data <- read_excel("data.xlsx", sheet = "Sheet1")
```

Step 4: Connecting to a Database

Relational databases like SQLite, MySQL, and PostgreSQL are commonly used to store large datasets. Connecting R to these databases allows you to query and retrieve data efficiently.

To demonstrate how this works without requiring you to set up a real database, we'll use an in-memory SQLite database (NOTE this works on a Windows 11 system but has not been tested on other systems). This database lives temporarily in your computer's memory and is deleted when you disconnect. It's perfect for testing and learning.

First install the packages needed.

```
R Code
options(repos = c(CRAN = "https://cran.r-project.org"))
# Install packages if needed
install.packages("DBI")
install.packages("RSQLite")


library(DBI)
library(RSQLite)
```

This line creates a new SQLite database that lives only in your computer's memory (not saved to disk). The connection object con is used to interact with this database. This setup is great for testing because the database disappears when you disconnect.

```
R Code
# Connect to an in-memory SQLite database
con <- dbConnect(RSQLite::SQLite(), ":memory:")
```

Here, we send a SQL command to the database to create a table called employees. The table has four columns. The first column, id, is a unique identifier for each employee and serves as the primary key. The second column, name, stores the employee's name as text. The third column, department, contains the name of the department where the employee works, also stored as text. Finally, the fourth column, salary, records the employee's salary as a real (decimal) number.

R Code

```
# Create a sample table named 'employees'
dbExecute(con, "
  CREATE TABLE employees (
    id INTEGER PRIMARY KEY,
    name TEXT,
    department TEXT,
    salary REAL
  )
")
```

Output

```
## [1] 0
```

This SQL command adds three rows to the employees table, one for each employee with their name, department, and salary.

R Code

```
# Insert some sample data
dbExecute(con, "
  INSERT INTO employees (name, department, salary) VALUES
  ('Alice', 'HR', 60000),
  ('Bob', 'IT', 75000),
  ('Charlie', 'Finance', 80000)
")
```

Output

```
## [1] 3
```

This command asks the database to list all the tables it contains. Since we only created one table, it should print "employees"

R Code
```
# List tables in the database
print(dbListTables(con))
```

Output
```
## [1] "employees"
```

This reads the full employees table from the database into an R data frame called employees_data. Printing it shows the table's contents in R.

R Code
```
# Read the 'employees' table into R
employees_data <- dbReadTable(con, "employees")
print(employees_data)
```

Output
```
##   id    name department
## 1  1   Alice         HR
## 2  2     Bob         IT
## 3  3 Charlie    Finance
##   salary
## 1  60000
## 2  75000
## 3  80000
```

This sends a SQL query to select only rows where the salary is above 65,000. The result is stored in high_earners and printed. It will show Bob and Charlie, since their salaries exceed 65,000.

```
R Code
# Run a custom SQL query to select
#   employees with salary > 65000
high_earners <- dbGetQuery(con,
    "SELECT * FROM employees WHERE salary > 65000")
print(high_earners)
```

```
Output
##    id    name department
## 1  2     Bob         IT
## 2  3 Charlie    Finance
##    salary
## 1   75000
## 2   80000
```

This closes the connection to the database and frees up resources. Since this is an in-memory database, all data is lost after disconnecting.

```
R Code
# Disconnect when done
dbDisconnect(con)
```

This example shows how to connect to a database, create tables, insert data, run queries, and disconnect properly without needing any external database setup. Using SQLite's in-memory mode is a great way to practice and test database operations directly within R.

Properly managing database connections ensures efficient and error-free access to your data. Typically, the role of maintaining data in a large organization is done by specialists in database management (usually computer science trained and not data analyst).

Wrap-Up

In this lab, you gained hands-on experience with some of the most important skills for working with data in R. You started by learning how to set and check your working directory, which helps R know where to look for files and where to save them. Then, you practiced importing and exporting data using CSV files—a common and widely used format. You also learned how to work with Excel files using special packages that handle Excel's structure. Finally you got an introduction to connecting R with relational databases, setting the stage for working with larger and more complex datasets in the future.

Exercises

Data Importing and Exporting

This exercise gives you practice working with three common data formats: CSV, Excel, and SQLite databases.

Dataset 1: Student Grades (CSV)

```
R Code
grades <- data.frame(
  student_id = 101:106,
  name = c("Anna", "Ben", "Cara", "Dan", "Ella", "Finn"),
  math = c(88, 75, 92, 85, 79, 95),
  english = c(90, 80, 91, 88, 84, 87)
)

# Write to CSV
write.csv(grades, "grades.csv", row.names = FALSE)
```

1. What is the average math score? Paste your code and result.
2. What is the average of English scores above 85?
3. Filter for students with math > 90 and save to a new CSV called `top_math.csv`. Paste the code used.
4. Read `top_math.csv` and print the contents. How many students are included?
5. In one sentence, why might a CSV file be easier to use than Excel in R?

Dataset 2: Inventory (Excel)

```
R Code
library(writexl)
library(readxl)

inventory <- data.frame(
  item = c("Pen", "Notebook", "Ruler", "Marker", "Eraser"),
  quantity = c(50, 100, 75, 40, 90),
  price = c(1.5, 3.2, 0.99, 2.0, 0.5)
)

# Write to Excel
write_xlsx(inventory, "inventory.xlsx")
```

6. What is the total inventory value (quantity × price summed across all items)?
7. Which item has the highest unit price?
8. Filter for items with quantity < 60 and save to `low_stock.xlsx`. Paste your code.
9. Read `low_stock.xlsx`, print the contents, and list the item names included.
10. In one sentence, describe a reason someone might prefer Excel over CSV for certain tasks.

Dataset 3: Museum Visitors (SQLite Database)

R Code

```
library(DBI)
library(RSQLite)


con <- dbConnect(SQLite(), ":memory:")


dbExecute(con, "
  CREATE TABLE visitors (
    visit_id INTEGER PRIMARY KEY,
    name TEXT,
    exhibit TEXT,
    duration_minutes INTEGER
  )
")
```

Output

```
## [1] 0
```

R Code

```
dbExecute(con, "
  INSERT INTO visitors (name, exhibit, duration_minutes) VALUES
  ('Alice', 'Dinosaurs', 45),
  ('Bob', 'Space', 60),
  ('Cara', 'Dinosaurs', 30),
  ('Dan', 'Art', 50),
  ('Ella', 'Space', 35)
")
```

Output

```
## [1] 5
```

Use dbReadTable() or dbGetQuery() to explore the database and answer.

11. What is the total time spent by all visitors in the "Dinosaurs" exhibit?
12. Write and run a SQL query to find visitors who spent more than 40 minutes. Paste your SQL and result.
13. In one sentence, explain why someone would use a database instead of a flat file like CSV or Excel.

Lab 14

Data Transformation and Manipulation

Data transformation and manipulation are essential steps in preparing raw data for meaningful analysis. This process involves changing the structure or content of your data by filtering, sorting, summarizing, and combining datasets. Mastering these skills helps you clean data, uncover patterns, and create focused views that make complex information easier to understand.

In this tutorial, we will use R's built-in mtcars dataset, which contains details about different car models, including horsepower, weight, and fuel efficiency. We will practice common data manipulation tasks.

Lesson Steps

Step 1: Load and Inspect the Dataset

The code first loads the built-in mtcars dataset, which contains data on various car models and their attributes such as miles per gallon, number of cylinders, horsepower, and more. Using the head() function displays the first six rows of this dataset.

R Code

```
data(mtcars)
head(mtcars)
```

Output

```
##                     mpg cyl
## Mazda RX4          21.0   6
## Mazda RX4 Wag      21.0   6
## Datsun 710         22.8   4
## Hornet 4 Drive     21.4   6
## Hornet Sportabout  18.7   8
## Valiant            18.1   6
##                    disp  hp
## Mazda RX4           160 110
## Mazda RX4 Wag       160 110
## Datsun 710          108  93
## Hornet 4 Drive      258 110
## Hornet Sportabout   360 175
## Valiant             225 105
##                    drat    wt
## Mazda RX4          3.90 2.620
## Mazda RX4 Wag      3.90 2.875
## Datsun 710         3.85 2.320
## Hornet 4 Drive     3.08 3.215
## Hornet Sportabout  3.15 3.440
## Valiant            2.76 3.460
##                    qsec vs am
## Mazda RX4          16.46  0  1
## Mazda RX4 Wag      17.02  0  1
## Datsun 710         18.61  1  1
## Hornet 4 Drive     19.44  1  0
```

```
## Hornet Sportabout 17.02  0  0
## Valiant             20.22  1  0
##                     gear carb
## Mazda RX4              4    4
## Mazda RX4 Wag          4    4
## Datsun 710             4    1
## Hornet 4 Drive         3    1
## Hornet Sportabout      3    2
## Valiant                3    1
```

Each row corresponds to a different car model, while each column represents a specific feature of the cars. For example, you will see columns for miles per gallon (mpg), number of cylinders (cyl), engine displacement (disp), horsepower (hp), weight (wt), and transmission type (am), among others.

Step 2: Filter Rows

Filtering data means selecting only the rows that meet specific conditions, allowing you to focus on a relevant subset of the dataset. This is especially useful when you want to limit your analysis to items that meet criteria such as a performance threshold, category, or range of values.

In the example, the filter keeps only cars with a miles per gallon (mpg) value greater than 25 narrowing the data down to more fuel-efficient vehicles. All other cars are excluded from the results. Filtering helps reduce noise and target your analysis more precisely.

R Code

```
# Filter cars with mpg > 25
cars_high_mpg <- mtcars[mtcars$mpg > 25, ]


# Show only car names and mpg values
print(head(cars_high_mpg[, "mpg", drop = FALSE]))
```

Output

```
##               mpg
## Fiat 128      32.4
## Honda Civic   30.4
## Toyota Corolla 33.9
## Fiat X1-9     27.3
## Porsche 914-2 26.0
## Lotus Europa  30.4
```

Step 3: Sort Rows

Sorting arranges the rows of a data set based on the values in one or more columns, either in ascending or descending order. This reordering does not remove any data but simply changes the position of rows to make patterns easier to see.

For example, sorting a dataset of cars by horsepower from highest to lowest lets you quickly identify the most powerful vehicles. Similarly, sorting miles per gallon in ascending order can highlight the least fuel-efficient models. Sorting is useful for ranking, comparing values, and spotting trends in your data.

R Code

```r
# Sort cars by horsepower (hp) in descending order
cars_sorted_hp <- mtcars[order(-mtcars$hp), ]


# Show only selected columns for the top results
head(cars_sorted_hp[, c("hp", "mpg", "wt")])
```

Output

```
##                      hp  mpg
## Maserati Bora       335 15.0
## Ford Pantera L      264 15.8
## Duster 360          245 14.3
## Camaro Z28          245 13.3
## Chrysler Imperial   230 14.7
## Lincoln Continental 215 10.4
##                        wt
## Maserati Bora        3.570
## Ford Pantera L       3.170
## Duster 360           3.570
## Camaro Z28           3.840
## Chrysler Imperial    5.345
## Lincoln Continental  5.424
```

Step 4: Aggregate (Summarize) Data

Aggregation is the process of summarizing detailed data into more mean-ingful values by applying calculations such as sums, averages, counts, min-imums, or maximums. This is especially useful when working with large datasets where you're more interested in overall trends than individual rows.

Aggregation often involves grouping the data by one or more categorical variables, then computing a summary statistic for each group. In addition most graphs are done on aggregated data and presentation summaries are as well.

This code calculates the average miles per gallon (mpg) for cars grouped by the number of cylinders (cyl) in the mtcars dataset. It uses the aggregate() function to group the data based on the cyl column and then computes the mean of the mpg values within each group. This results in a new summary table that shows the average fuel efficiency for cars with 4, 6, and 8 cylinders, allowing for easy comparison between engine types.

R Code
```
# Calculate average mpg by number of cylinders
avg_mpg_by_cyl <- aggregate(mpg ~ cyl,
         data = mtcars, FUN = mean)
print(avg_mpg_by_cyl)
```

Output
```
##    cyl      mpg
## 1    4 26.66364
## 2    6 19.74286
## 3    8 15.10000
```

Step 5: Join / Merge Data

Joining, or merging, is the process of combining data from two or more tables based on a shared column, often called a key. This allows you to bring together related information that is stored separately, enriching your dataset with additional variables.

This code shows how to merge two data frames in R by using a common column (an identity key, required to do joins effectively), which here is the car model. The first data frame, cars_info, is created from the built-in mtcars dataset and contains two columns: model, taken from the row names of mtcars, and mpg. The second data frame, car_type, is smaller and manually lists the models of two specific cars along with their types. The merge() function combines these two data frames based on the model column. Only the rows with matching model names in both data frames will be included in the merged result.

```
R Code
# Create two small data frames
cars_info <- data.frame(model = rownames(mtcars),
                        mpg = mtcars$mpg)
car_type <- data.frame(model = c("Mazda RX4", "Datsun 710"),
                        type = c("sports", "compact"))
print(cars_info)
```

Output

```
##                       model  mpg
## 1               Mazda RX4 21.0
## 2           Mazda RX4 Wag 21.0
## 3              Datsun 710 22.8
## 4          Hornet 4 Drive 21.4
## 5       Hornet Sportabout 18.7
## 6                 Valiant 18.1
## 7              Duster 360 14.3
## 8               Merc 240D 24.4
## 9                Merc 230 22.8
## 10               Merc 280 19.2
## 11              Merc 280C 17.8
## 12             Merc 450SE 16.4
## 13             Merc 450SL 17.3
## 14            Merc 450SLC 15.2
## 15     Cadillac Fleetwood 10.4
## 16    Lincoln Continental 10.4
## 17      Chrysler Imperial 14.7
## 18               Fiat 128 32.4
## 19             Honda Civic 30.4
## 20          Toyota Corolla 33.9
## 21           Toyota Corona 21.5
## 22         Dodge Challenger 15.5
## 23             AMC Javelin 15.2
## 24              Camaro Z28 13.3
## 25        Pontiac Firebird 19.2
## 26               Fiat X1-9 27.3
## 27           Porsche 914-2 26.0
## 28            Lotus Europa 30.4
## 29           Ford Pantera L 15.8
```

164

```
## 30          Ferrari Dino 19.7
## 31          Maserati Bora 15.0
## 32             Volvo 142E 21.4
```

R Code
```
print(car_type)
```

Output
```
##          model      type
## 1  Mazda RX4    sports
## 2 Datsun 710 compact
```

R Code
```
# Merge based on 'model'
combined_data <- merge(cars_info, car_type, by = "model")
print(combined_data)
```

Output
```
##          model  mpg      type
## 1 Datsun 710 22.8 compact
## 2  Mazda RX4 21.0  sports
```

Step 6: Subset Columns

When working with large datasets, it's often helpful to narrow your focus to just the columns relevant to your analysis. Subsetting columns lets you create a smaller, more manageable dataset by selecting only the variables (features) you need. This can make your code clearer and speed up processing.

For example, the code below keeps only the mpg (miles per gallon) and hp (horsepower) columns from the mtcars dataset, so you can focus on fuel efficiency and engine power.

```
R Code
# Keep only 'mpg' and 'hp' columns
subset_data <- mtcars[, c("mpg", "hp")]
head(subset_data)
```

```
Output
##                    mpg  hp
## Mazda RX4          21.0 110
## Mazda RX4 Wag      21.0 110
## Datsun 710         22.8  93
## Hornet 4 Drive     21.4 110
## Hornet Sportabout  18.7 175
## Valiant            18.1 105
```

Wrap-Up

In this lab, you practiced essential data transformation and manipulation techniques that are fundamental for effective data analysis. You learned how to filter rows to focus on the most relevant data, enabling more targeted insights. Sorting the data helped you identify important patterns and trends by arranging records based on specific criteria. Aggregation allowed you to summarize information at the group level, making it easier to understand overall characteristics within categories. You also explored merging datasets, which combines related information from multiple sources into a single, richer dataset. Finally, subsetting columns helped you narrow your focus to only the variables needed for your analysis, simplifying your workflow.

Exercises

Data Transformation and Manipulation

Data transformation and manipulation are the skills practiced in this exercise including filtering, sorting, aggregating and subsetting.

Dataset A: Employee Performance

This dataset records key performance indicators for employees in a small company.

```
R Code
# Dataset A: Employee performance

employee_data <- data.frame(
  name = c("Alice", "Bob", "Carol", "David",
          "Eva", "Frank"),
  department = c("HR", "IT", "IT", "Marketing",
          "HR", "Marketing"),
  rating = c(4.2, 3.8, 4.5, 3.0, 4.0, 3.6),
  salary = c(55000, 62000, 60000, 58000, 53000, 57000)
)
```

1. Filter the dataset to show only employees with a rating above 4. Paste the code and output.

2. Sort the employees by salary from highest to lowest. Paste the output and name the highest-paid employee.

3. Calculate the average salary for each department. Paste the summary table and identify which department has the highest average.

4. Create a second dataset that includes each employee's name and whether they are full-time or part-time. Merge this with the employee dataset and show the result.

5. Subset the dataset to keep only the name and rating columns. Paste the result.

Dataset B: Online Course Participation

This dataset represents user behavior in an online course.

```
R Code
# Dataset B: Online course activity

course_data <- data.frame(
  username = c(
    "jane_d", "mike_t", "sara_k", "li_zhang",
    "anil_r", "nina_m"
  ),
  study_hours = c(12, 4, 15, 7, 10, 8),
  completed_quiz1 = c(
    TRUE, FALSE, TRUE, TRUE,
    FALSE, TRUE
  ),
  learning_style = c(
    "visual", "auditory", "visual",
    "reading",
    "auditory", "visual"
  )
)
```

6. Filter the dataset to show only students who studied more than 10

hours. Paste the code and result.

7. Sort the dataset by study_hours in descending order. Who studied the most, and what is their learning style?

8. Calculate the average study_hours grouped by learning_style. Paste the result.

9. Create a second dataset with usernames and their preferred device (e.g., "mobile", "desktop"). Merge it with the course dataset. Paste the merged result.

10. Subset the course dataset to include only the username, study_hours, and completed_quiz1 columns. Paste the result.

Dataset C: Product Sales

This dataset tracks sales transactions in a small store.

```
R Code
# Dataset C: Product sales
sales_data <- data.frame(
  product = c("pen", "notebook", "pen", "eraser",
             "notebook", "pen", "eraser"),
  price = c(1.50, 3.00, 1.50, 0.75, 3.00, 1.50, 0.75),
  quantity = c(10, 5, 20, 15, 3, 5, 10),
  store = c("A", "A", "B", "A", "B", "B", "A")
)
```

11. Calculate the total quantity sold by product. Which product sold the most?

12. Create a new column called revenue (price × quantity). Then calculate the total revenue by store and sort it from highest to lowest.

13. Filter the dataset to show only transactions for the product "notebook". Paste the result.

14. Create a second dataset mapping each store to its location (e.g., "urban", "rural"). Merge it with the sales dataset and paste the merged result.

15. Subset the sales dataset to keep only the product, quantity, and store columns. Paste the result.

Lab 15

Introduction to SQL

SQL (Structured Query Language) is a programming language designed to interact with data stored in relational databases. These databases organize data into tables, like spreadsheets, and SQL lets us write commands to search, filter, and combine this data quickly and efficiently.

SQL is widely used in data analytics, business, and technology because most organizations rely on databases to store their information. Learning SQL helps you explore data, solve problems, and make informed decisions.

In this lab, we'll practice SQL queries in R using the `sqldf` package, which lets you run SQL on data frames.

Lesson Steps

Step 1: Load Packages and Create Sample Data

First, install and load the sqldf package (if you haven't already), then create two example data frames.

173

R Code
```
options(repos = c(CRAN = "https://cran.r-project.org"))
# Install sqldf if needed (run once)
install.packages("sqldf")


# Load sqldf
library(sqldf)
```

R Code
```
# Create data
# Customers table
customers <- data.frame(
  customer_id = c(1, 2, 3, 4),
  name = c("Alice", "Bob", "Carol", "Dave"),
  city = c("New York", "Chicago", "New York", "Boston")
)


# Sales table
sales <- data.frame(
  transaction_id = 101:104,
  customer_id = c(1, 2, 1, 3),
  amount = c(150, 90, 200, 50)
)


# View the tables
customers
```

Output
```
##    customer_id  name      city
## 1            1 Alice New York
## 2            2   Bob  Chicago
## 3            3 Carol New York
## 4            4  Dave   Boston
```

R Code
```
sales
```

Output
```
##    transaction_id customer_id
## 1            101           1
## 2            102           2
## 3            103           1
## 4            104           3
##    amount
## 1    150
## 2     90
## 3    200
## 4     50
```

Step 2: Basic SELECT Query

When working with databases or large tables, it's often important to extract only the information you need rather than loading entire datasets. The SELECT statement in SQL is used to retrieve specific columns from a table, allowing you to focus on relevant data and reduce unnecessary processing.

175

In the example code, the sqldf package in R runs a simple SQL query on a data frame named customers. The query "SELECT name, city FROM customers" tells R to extract only the name and city columns from the customers table. This returns a smaller table with just those two columns, making it easier to view or analyze key information without extra data.

```
R Code
# Select name and city from customers
sqldf("SELECT name, city FROM customers")
```

```
Output
##     name       city
## 1 Alice  New York
## 2    Bob   Chicago
## 3 Carol  New York
## 4   Dave    Boston
```

Step 3: Join Two Tables

In data analysis, it's common to have related information stored in separate tables. For example, you might have one table with customer details and another with their sales records. To analyze the data effectively, you often need to combine these tables into one, matching rows based on a common key—in this case, customer_id. This process is called joining tables.

The provided code uses the sqldf package in R to perform an SQL join between two tables: customers and sales. The query selects the customer's name from the customers table and the sales amount from the sales table. It joins the tables where the customer_id values match in both tables.

R Code
```
# Join customers and sales on customer_id
sqldf("
  SELECT customers.name, sales.amount
  FROM customers
  JOIN sales ON customers.customer_id = sales.customer_id
")
```

Output
```
##      name amount
## 1 Alice    150
## 2 Alice    200
## 3   Bob     90
## 4 Carol     50
```

The result is a new table showing each customer's name alongside their corresponding sales amount. This allows you to see how much each customer has spent, combining information from both sources in one view.

Step 4: Filtering with WHERE

When working with data, it's often necessary not only to combine information from multiple tables but also to filter the results based on specific conditions. The SQL WHERE clause allows you to select only those rows that meet a certain criterion, making your queries more targeted and efficient.

In this example, the R code uses the sqldf package to join two tables—customers and sales—based on the shared customer_id. It retrieves the customer's name and the corresponding sales but only includes those sales where the amount is greater than $100.

177

The query combines the data from both tables using an inner join, then filters the rows with the WHERE clause to keep only higher-value sales.

```
R Code
# Show sales over $100
sqldf("
  SELECT customers.name, sales.amount
  FROM customers
  JOIN sales ON customers.customer_id = sales.customer_id
  WHERE sales.amount > 100
")
```

```
Output
##      name amount
## 1 Alice    150
## 2 Alice    200
```

The result is a filtered table showing customers who made purchases ex-
ceeding $100.

Step 5: Advanced Filtering (AND, OR, LIKE)

AND

Advanced filtering in SQL allows you to refine your queries by combining
multiple conditions using logical operators like AND and OR. This enables
you to select only the rows that meet all (or some) specified criteria, making
your data retrieval more precise and tailored to your analysis needs.

For example, the following SQL query selects customers who have made
sales greater than $100 and who live in New York. It joins the customers and

sales tables using the common customer_id key and then applies the WHERE clause with two conditions combined by AND. Only customers meeting both criteria—high sales and residing in New York—are included in the results.

```
R Code
# Sales over $100 AND customer city is New York
sqldf("
  SELECT customers.name, sales.amount
  FROM customers
  JOIN sales ON customers.customer_id = sales.customer_id
  WHERE sales.amount > 100 AND customers.city = 'New York'
")
```

```
Output
##      name amount
## 1 Alice    150
## 2 Alice    200
```

Both conditions (sales greater than $100 and who live in New York) must be true to appear in results.

LIKE

In advanced filtering, the LIKE operator is used to search for patterns within text columns. It allows you to match partial strings using wildcards, making it useful for flexible text filtering when you don't know the exact value or want to find all entries fitting a certain pattern.

In this example, the SQL query selects all customers whose names start with the letter "A". The % wildcard represents any sequence of characters (including none), so 'A%' means "any name beginning with 'A' followed by zero or more characters."

```
R Code
# Names starting with 'A'
sqldf("SELECT * FROM customers WHERE name LIKE 'A%'")
```

```
Output
##    customer_id  name      city
## 1            1 Alice New York
```

This query returns all rows from the customers table where the name column starts with "A", helping you quickly filter based on name patterns.

Wrap-Up

In this lab, you learned how to write basic SQL SELECT queries to retrieve specific data from tables. You practiced joining tables on common keys to combine related information into a single dataset. Additionally, you explored how to filter data using the WHERE clause, applying both simple and multiple conditions to narrow down results. You also learned how to use pattern matching with the LIKE operator, which allows for flexible text filtering based on partial matches.

Exercises

Introduction to SQL

These exercises practice using SQL in R with the `sqldf` package. You will write queries to extract specific columns, join tables using a shared key, filter rows using conditions, and match text patterns.

Dataset 1: Library Inventory and Borrowing Records

This dataset contains information about books in a library and records of which books were borrowed.

```
R Code
# Load package
library(sqldf)

# Book inventory
books <- data.frame(
  book_id = 1:5,
  title = c("Data Science 101", "Intro to R", "Advanced SQL",
            "Machine Learning", "Visualization Guide"),
  author = c("Smith", "Jones", "Lee", "Chen", "Taylor"),
  genre = c("Data", "R", "SQL", "ML", "Graphics")
)

# Borrowing records
borrowed <- data.frame(
  borrow_id = 201:205,
  book_id = c(1, 2, 1, 3, 5),
  borrower = c("Eva", "Liam", "Eva", "Noah", "Sophia"),
  days_borrowed = c(14, 7, 21, 10, 5)
)
```

1. Write an SQL query to select the title and genre from the books table. Paste the query and result.

2. Write an SQL query to select all columns from the borrowed table. Paste the result.

3. Join the books and borrowed tables using book_id. Select the title and borrower. Paste the result.

4. Modify the previous query to show only records where the book was borrowed for more than 10 days.

5. Which book title has been borrowed more than once? Write a query to group by title and count borrows.

Dataset 2: Restaurant Orders and Menu

This dataset represents a restaurant's menu and the orders placed by customers.

```
R Code
# Menu table
menu <- data.frame(
  item_id = 101:106,
  item_name = c("Burger", "Salad", "Pizza", "Soup",
                "Pasta", "Taco"),
  price = c(8.5, 6.0, 10.0, 5.5, 9.0, 7.0)
)


# Orders table
orders <- data.frame(
  order_id = 301:306,
  item_id = c(101, 103, 102, 106, 101, 105),
  customer = c("Mike", "Anna", "Nina", "Leo", "Mike", "Tina"),
  quantity = c(1, 2, 1, 3, 2, 1)
)
```

6. Write an SQL query to return the customer and item_name from a join of menu and orders. Paste the result.

7. Modify the previous query to include only orders where the quantity is greater than 1.

8. Write a query to calculate the total cost per order using price * quantity. Show customer, item_name, and total_cost.

9. Use LIKE to return any items from the menu that contain the letter 'a' anywhere in the name.

10. Which customer placed the most expensive total order? Use ORDER BY to find the highest total and identify them.

Lab 16

Unsupervised Learning (Clustering)

Machine learning is a powerful tool for finding patterns, making predictions, grouping similar items, and even automating decisions. It allows us to extract insights from large amounts of data—far more quickly and efficiently than a human could on their own.

There are two main categories of machine learning: supervised learning and unsupervised learning. In supervised learning, we train a model using data that already includes the correct answers. For example, we might have a dataset of customer information along with whether each customer made a purchase. Using this data, we can train a model to predict whether future customers are likely to buy something. The key feature of supervised learning is that we start with labeled data—examples where the outcome is already known (purchase vs no purchase).

In contrast, unsupervised learning is used when we don't have labeled data. Our goal is to find hidden patterns or groupings in that data. Rather than teaching the machine by example, we ask it to explore and make sense of the data on its own. This is especially useful in the early stages of data analysis, when we might not yet know what to look for or what kinds of patterns might exist.

In this lab, we focus on unsupervised learning. You will explore three com-

185

mon and useful techniques for uncovering structure in unlabeled data: K-Means clustering, hierarchical clustering, and DBSCAN.

Lesson Steps

Clustering with K-Means

K-Means clustering is a widely used unsupervised learning method that groups similar data points into distinct clusters. The main goal of this technique is to organize data in such a way that items within the same cluster are as similar as possible, while those in different clusters are as different as possible.

The process begins by selecting the number of clusters you want to find—commonly referred to as K. For example, you might choose to divide your data into 2 or 3 clusters. Next, the algorithm initializes cluster centers, known as centroids, which may be randomly chosen or based on some strategy. Each data point is then assigned to the nearest centroid, creating initial groupings.

Once all points have been assigned, the centroids are recalculated based on the current members of each cluster. The process of assigning points to the closest centroid and updating the centroids continues in cycles until the cluster assignments stabilize—meaning they no longer change from one iteration to the next. This iterative refinement helps the algorithm converge on a stable set of clusters that best represent the structure in the data.

K-Means clustering has numerous applications In marketing, it can help businesses segment customers based on behavior or preferences. In biology, it can classify gene expression patterns. In image processing, it can group similar colors for image compression or enhancement.

Step 1: Simulate customer data (K-Means)

To explore K means we begin by simulating a small dataset that represents customer behavior.

```
R Code
# Set seed for reproducibility
set.seed(123)

# Create a small customer dataset
customers <- data.frame(
  Visits = c(1, 2, 1, 8, 9, 10),
  Spend = c(20, 22, 19, 200, 210, 190)
)

# View data
print(customers)
```

```
Output
##    Visits Spend
## 1      1    20
## 2      2    22
## 3      1    19
## 4      8   200
## 5      9   210
## 6     10   190
```

Step 2: Apply K-Means Clustering (K-Means)

In this step, we apply the K-Means clustering algorithm to our customer dataset. kmeans(customers, centers = 2) tells R to group the customers into two clusters based on the two variables—Visits and Spend.

The result of this operation is stored in an object called k_model. This object contains several important pieces of information. One key component is k_model$cluster, which shows the cluster assignment for each customer— either cluster 1 or cluster 2.

By running print(k_model$cluster), we can see exactly how each customer was grouped—revealing whether they were placed in the first or second cluster.

R Code
```
# Perform K-means with 2 clusters
k_model <- kmeans(customers, centers = 2)

# View cluster assignment
print(k_model$cluster)
```

Output
```
## [1] 1 1 1 2 2 2
```

This is where the machine learning aspect of K-Means happens. It allows us to uncover natural segments in the data, such as identifying which customers behave alike and may respond to similar marketing strategies.

Step 3: Visualize the Clusters (K-Means)

Now we can create a visual representation of the customer data using a scatter plot.

```
R Code
# Plot customers with cluster colors
plot(customers, col = k_model$cluster, pch = 19,
     main = "K-Means Clustering: Customer Segments")
```

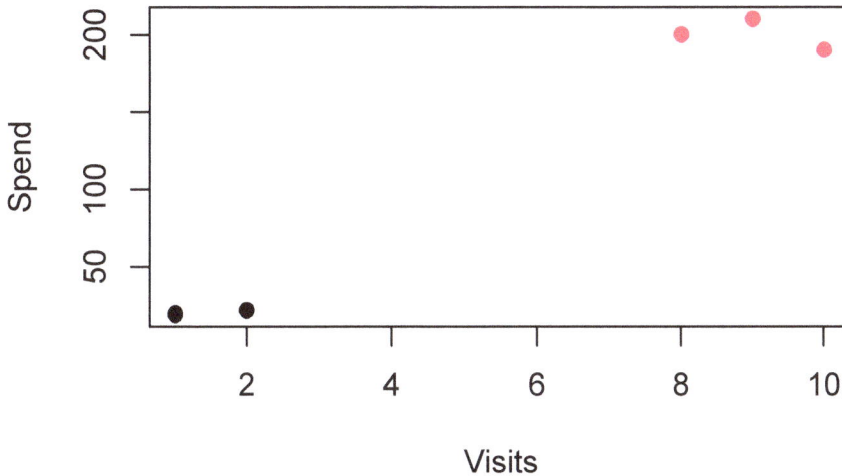

K-Means Clustering: Customer Segments

Visualizing the results of clustering is important because it allows you to quickly assess how well the algorithm performed.

Hierarchical Clustering

Hierarchical clustering is another popular method for grouping similar data points, but it works differently from K-Means. Instead of specifying the number of clusters upfront, hierarchical clustering builds a tree-like structure called a dendrogram that shows how data points can be grouped step-by-step based on their similarity.

The method calculates a distance matrix, which measures the pairwise distances between every data point. This matrix quantifies how close or far apart points are from each other. The hierarchical clustering algorithm then uses this distance matrix to progressively merge the closest pairs of points or clusters. This results in a dendrogram — a tree diagram that visually represents the nested grouping of points from individual data points up to one single cluster that contains all points. By looking at the dendrogram, you can decide how many clusters to cut out by selecting a level where groups are clearly separated.

Compared to K-Means, hierarchical clustering doesn't require you to choose the number of clusters at the start. Hierarchical clustering can be more computationally intensive with larger datasets, while K-Means is generally faster and more scalable.

Step 4: Generate sample data

In this step, we create a small set of six random data points in two dimensions. Each point is labeled from P1 to P6 for easy identification. This sample data will serve as the basis for demonstrating how hierarchical clustering groups similar points based on their distances.

R Code

```
# Create 6 random data points in 2D
data <- matrix(rnorm(12), ncol = 2)
rownames(data) <- paste0("P", 1:6)

# View data
print(data)
```

Output

```
##             [,1]          [,2]
## P1 -1.6895557 -1.7272706
## P2  1.2394959  1.6901844
## P3 -0.1089660  0.5038124
## P4 -0.1172420  2.5283366
## P5  0.1830826  0.5490967
## P6  1.2805549  0.2382129
```

Step 5: Compute distance matrix (Hierarchical)

Here, we calculate the distance matrix, which measures how far apart each pair of data points is from one another. The dist() function computes these distances based on the values in the dataset. This matrix provides the information needed to determine which points or groups of points are closest and should be merged first.

R Code

```
# Compute distances
dist_mat <- dist(data)


# View
dist_mat
```

Output

```
##              P1         P2
## P2 4.5009267
## P3 2.7342267 1.7960589
## P4 4.5367789 1.5947529
## P5 2.9476469 1.5550209
## P6 3.5615562 1.4525519
##              P3         P4
## P2
## P3
## P4 2.0245410
## P5 0.2955386 2.0018954
## P6 1.4146771 2.6830025
##              P5
## P2
## P3
## P4
## P5
## P6 1.1406551
```

Step 6: Apply clustering (Hierarchical)

In this step, the hierarchical clustering algorithm is applied. The hclust() function performs the clustering by successively merging the closest data points or clusters based on their distances. The result is stored in the object hc, which contains the full hierarchy of cluster merges.

We then visualize the result with a dendrogram using the plot() function. The dendrogram is a tree-like diagram that shows how data points are grouped together at different levels of similarity.

R Code
```
# Hierarchical clustering
hc <- hclust(dist_mat)


# Plot dendrogram
plot(hc, main = "Hierarchical Clustering Dendrogram")
```

Hierarchical Clustering Dendrogram

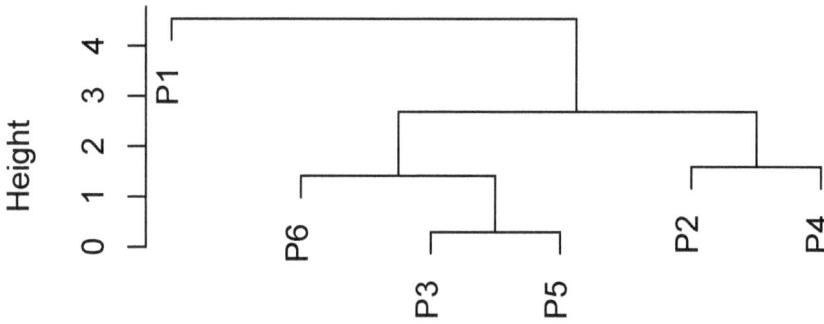

dist_mat
hclust (*, "complete")

Clustering with DBSCAN

DBSCAN (Density-Based Spatial Clustering of Applications with Noise) is a clustering method that groups together data points that are closely packed, forming dense regions, while identifying points in sparse areas as noise or outliers. Unlike K-Means, which requires you to specify the number of clusters beforehand and assumes clusters are roughly spherical, DBSCAN discovers clusters of any shape based on the density of points.

Compared to hierarchical clustering, which builds a tree of clusters showing relationships at all levels but doesn't handle noise explicitly, DBSCAN automatically detects outliers and does not need the number of clusters to be specified in advance. This makes DBSCAN especially useful for datasets where clusters are irregularly shaped or when identifying noise is important.

Step 7: Load the package (DBSCAN)

Before using DBSCAN for clustering, you need to load the dbscan package in R. If it's not already installed, you can install it first. This package provides the functions needed to perform density-based clustering and analyze your data.

```
R Code
options(repos = c(CRAN = "https://cran.r-project.org"))
# Install if needed
install.packages("dbscan")
library(dbscan)
```

Step 8: Create a dataset (DBSCAN)

In this step, we create a simple dataset with two clear clusters. Each row represents a point in two-dimensional space. This example data will help demonstrate how DBSCAN groups points based on their density and identifies clusters in the dataset.

R Code

```
# Create a dataset with 2 clusters
data <- matrix(c(
  1, 2,
  1.5, 2,
  2, 2,
  8, 8,
  8.5, 8,
  9, 8
), ncol = 2, byrow = TRUE)


# View data
print(data)
```

Output

```
##        [,1] [,2]
## [1,]   1.0    2
## [2,]   1.5    2
## [3,]   2.0    2
## [4,]   8.0    8
## [5,]   8.5    8
## [6,]   9.0    8
```

Step 9: Run DBSCAN

Apply the DBSCAN algorithm to the dataset using the dbscan() function. The eps parameter sets the radius around each point to look for neighbors, while minPts defines the minimum number of points required to form a dense region (a cluster).

By printing db$cluster, we can see the cluster assignment for each point, where numbers indicate cluster membership and zeros represent noise points. This output shows how DBSCAN has identified groups and isolated outliers in the data.

R Code
```
# Apply DBSCAN with epsilon radius and minimum points
db <- dbscan(data, eps = 1.5, minPts = 2)

# View cluster results
print(db$cluster)
```

Output
```
## [1] 1 1 1 2 2 2
```

Step 10: Plot the DBSCAN result

This step creates a scatter plot to visualize the clustering results from DB-SCAN.

R Code
```
# Visualize the DBSCAN clustering
plot(data, col = db$cluster + 1, pch = 19,
     main = "DBSCAN Clustering")
```

DBSCAN Clustering

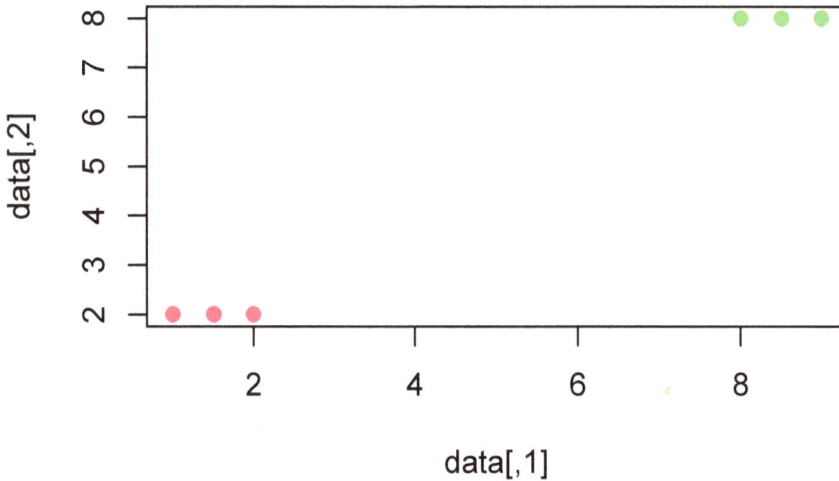

Wrap-Up

In this lab, we explored three popular clustering methods—K-Means, Hierarchical Clustering, and DBSCAN—to group similar data points based on their features.

K-Means required us to specify the number of clusters upfront and grouped data by minimizing distances to cluster centroids. Hierarchical clustering built a dendrogram that showed nested groupings and allowed us to explore clusters at different levels without predefining their number. DBSCAN, on the other hand, grouped points based on density, automatically detecting clusters of any shape and identifying noise points without needing the number of clusters in advance.

Visualizing results with scatter plots and dendrograms helped us understand how each method organizes data and highlights patterns. This lab provided a practical foundation for choosing the right clustering technique to use to make patterns from unlabelled data.

Exercises

Clustering (Unsupervised Learning)

These exercise practice K-Means, Hierarchical Clustering, and DBSCAN.

Dataset A: Animal Movement Patterns

This dataset tracks how far and how frequently animals moved during observation sessions.

```
R Code
# Set seed for reproducibility
set.seed(42)


# Simulate movement data for 8 animals
movement <- data.frame(
  Distance = c(100, 110, 95, 5, 7, 6, 102, 4),
  Frequency = c(30, 25, 27, 3, 4, 2, 28, 5)
)
```

1. Apply K-Means clustering with `centers` = 2 to the `movement` dataset. Paste your R code and show the resulting cluster assignments.

2. What does each cluster likely represent in terms of movement behavior?

3. Create a scatterplot of the data colored by cluster. What do you notice about the separation?

4. Change the number of clusters to `centers` = 3. What changes, and does it give a more meaningful grouping?

5. What role does the scale of `Distance` and `Frequency` play in cluster-

ing here? (Bonus: Try `scale(movement)` and repeat K-Means—what changes?)

Dataset B: Bat Acoustic Signals

This dataset simulates three acoustic features measured from bat calls in a sound lab.

```
R Code
# Simulate bat acoustic signal data
set.seed(2025)

bats <- data.frame(
  Pitch = c(22, 23, 22.5, 80, 78, 82, 55, 57),
  Duration = c(0.2, 0.22, 0.21, 0.8, 0.75, 0.82,
               0.5, 0.55),
  Intensity = c(35, 36, 34, 70, 68, 72, 50, 52)
)
```

6. Compute the Euclidean distance matrix for the bat data. What does this matrix tell you?

7. Apply hierarchical clustering to the dataset and plot a dendrogram. Paste your code and the dendrogram.

8. Based on the dendrogram, how many clusters would you choose and why?

9. Use `cutree()` to assign each observation to a cluster (cut into 2 or 3). What are the cluster labels?

10. What features seem to drive the separation among clusters in this dataset?

Dataset C: Nesting Site Coordinates

```
R Code
# Simulated GPS-like data for bird nesting sites
nest_sites <- matrix(c(
  1, 2,  1.2, 2.1,  1.1, 1.9,
  6, 5.9,  6.1, 6,  6.2, 6.1,
  10, 1,  10.2, 1.1
), ncol = 2, byrow = TRUE)
```

11. Plot the nesting site coordinates. Do any visible clusters appear?

12. Run DBSCAN with eps = 0.5 and minPts = 2. What clusters are dis-covered? Paste the cluster labels.

13. Try a larger eps = 1.0. How do the clusters change?

14. Which points (if any) are classified as noise? What does this mean?

15. What are the strengths of DBSCAN over K-Means for this type of spatial data?

Lab 17

Supervised Learning (Classification)

Introduction

Supervised learning is one of the main types of machine learning and plays a central role in many AI systems. In supervised learning, we work with labeled data—data where we know both the input and the correct output. A label is the known outcome assigned to each data point in supervised learning, which is typically a category (like "spam," "promotion," or "social"). Labels typically are in the data already or can come from a first step of clustering and then assigning a label based on clustering. The goal is to train a model that can learn from these examples and accurately predict outcomes (labels) for new, unseen data.

In this unit, we focus on classification problems, where the model learns to assign data to categories such as "yes" or "no," or "Class A" vs. "Class B." We'll introduce several major classification techniques used in supervised learning, including decision trees, support vector machines, and k-nearest neighbors.

Lesson Steps

Classification – Decision Tree

A decision tree is a classification model that uses a flowchart-like structure to make predictions based on feature values. It splits data into branches depending on the conditions of the input variables. Each internal node represents a decision based on a feature, and each leaf node represents a final prediction. Decision trees are intuitive and easy to interpret, making them a common starting point for classification tasks.

Step 1: Create a Dataset

We begin by creating a small dataset that includes three variables: Weather, Temp, and Exercise. Each row represents a specific day with weather conditions and if the person exercised. This setup allows us to train a model that can learn how weather and temperature influence the decision to exercise.

```
R Code
# Create example dataset
data <- data.frame(
  Weather = c("Sunny", "Sunny", "Rainy", "Sunny",
              "Rainy", "Sunny", "Rainy", "Rainy",
              "Sunny", "Rainy", "Sunny", "Rainy",
              "Sunny", "Rainy", "Cloudy", "Cloudy",
              "Sunny", "Rainy", "Cloudy", "Sunny"),
  Temp = c("Hot", "Cold", "Cold", "Hot", "Hot",
           "Cold", "Cold", "Hot", "Cold", "Hot",
           "Cold", "Cold", "Hot", "Cold", "Cold",
           "Hot", "Hot", "Cold",  "Hot", "Cold"),
  Exercise = c("No", "Yes", "No", "No", "No", "Yes",
               "Yes", "No", "Yes","No", "Yes", "No",
               "No", "Yes", "Yes", "No", "No", "Yes",
               "No", "Yes")
)
```

Step 2: Load Required Packages

To build and visualize the decision tree, we need to install and load the appropriate R packages. The rpart (recursive partition) package provides functions to build the tree, while rpart.plot helps us create a clear and readable visual of the tree structure.

```
R Code
options(repos = c(CRAN = "https://cran.r-project.org"))
# Install and load necessary packages
install.packages("rpart")
install.packages("rpart.plot")


library(rpart)
library(rpart.plot)
```

Step 3: Train the Decision Tree Model

We will use the rpart() function to train our model. Set Exercise as the outcome variable we want to predict and Weather and Temp as predictor (input) variables. The method = "class" argument tells R that this is a classification task. The model analyzes the dataset and finds the best way to split the data into branches that lead to accurate predictions.

```
R Code
# Train the decision tree model
tree_model <- rpart(Exercise ~ Weather + Temp,
                    data = data, method = "class")
```

Step 4: Visualize the Tree

The model needs to be visualized to make sense. For this we use rpart.plot(). This plot shows the tree's decision process step-by-step. Each split in the tree represents a question about the input variables, and each final node gives a prediction—either "Yes" or "No" for exercise.

R Code

```
# Plot the decision tree
rpart.plot(tree_model)
```

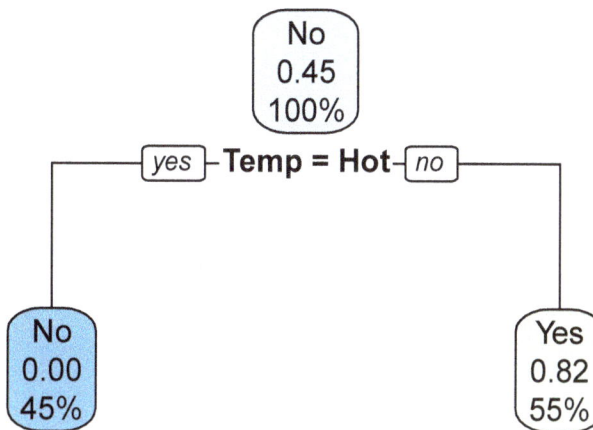

```
         ┌─────────┐
         │   No    │
         │  0.45   │
         │  100%   │
         └─────────┘
      ┌yes├─Temp = Hot─┤no├────────────┐
      │                                 │
┌─────────┐                      ┌─────────┐
│   No    │                      │   Yes   │
│  0.00   │                      │  0.82   │
│  45%    │                      │  55%    │
└─────────┘                      └─────────┘
```

Classification – Support Vector Machines (SVM)

Support Vector Machines (SVM) is a popular supervised learning method used for classification tasks. It works by finding the best possible boundary (called a hyperplane) that separates data points of different classes. SVM is particularly powerful when the classes are clearly separated.

Step 5: Create a small dataset

First, we create a simple dataset with two features (X1 and X2) and a target class variable with two categories, "A" and "B."

```
R Code
# Create small dataset
df <- data.frame(
  X1 = c(2, 3, 10, 11),
  X2 = c(2, 3, 10, 11),
  Class = as.factor(c("A", "A", "B", "B"))
)
```

Step 6: Install and load the SVM package

We use the e1071 package in R, which provides functions to train SVM models.

```
R Code
# Install and load e1071 package
install.packages("e1071")
library(e1071)
```

Step 7: Train the SVM model

Using the dataset, train the SVM model to classify the data points into classes "A" or "B" based on features X1 and X2.

```
R Code
# Train the SVM model
svm_model <- svm(Class ~ X1 + X2, data = df)
```

Step 8: Visualize the SVM decision boundary

Finally, plot the dataset and the decision boundary created by the SVM model to see how it separates the two classes.

```
R Code
# Plot SVM decision boundary

plot(svm_model, df,
     col = c("#637D8D", "#EE6C4D"),
     symbolPalette = c("#637D8D", "#EE6C4D"),
     svSymbol = 17,
     dataSymbol = 16,
     grid = 150)
```

SVM classification plot

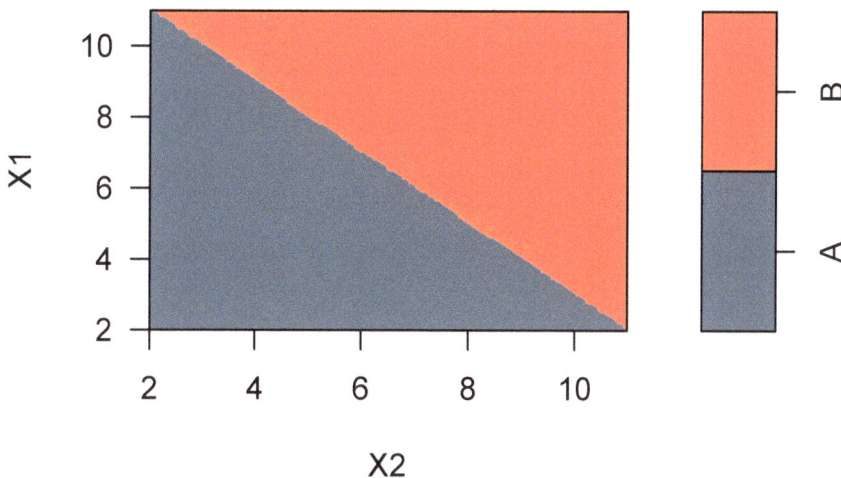

Classification - k-Nearest Neighbors (k-NN)

k-Nearest Neighbors (k-NN) is one of the simplest and most intuitive supervised learning algorithms used for classification. The core idea behind k-NN is that similar data points tend to be near each other in the feature space.

When we want to classify a new, unlabeled data point, the algorithm looks at the 'k' closest points from the training data (where 'k' is a user-chosen number). Nearby points are called the neighbors. For classification problems, k-NN assigns the new point the label that is most common among its neighbors, which is known as a majority vote. This approach makes no assumptions about the underlying data distribution and is easy to understand and implement.

Step 9: Load the library

To perform k-nearest neighbors (KNN) classification in R, we'll use the class package.

```
R Code
options(repos = c(CRAN = "https://cran.r-project.org"))
install.packages('class')
library(class)
```

Step 10: Create example data

Let's create a simple dataset that includes height and weight measurements, along with labels that classify each individual as either "Short" or "Tall." We also define a new data point (a person with height 66 and weight 130) that we want to classify based on the existing training examples.

```
R Code
# Training data
train_data <- data.frame(
  height = c(60, 62, 65, 72, 75, 78),
  weight = c(115, 120, 130, 160, 175, 200)
)


# Labels for training data
train_labels <- c("Short", "Short", "Short",
                  "Tall", "Tall", "Tall")

# New data point to classify
test_data <- data.frame(
  height = c(66),
  weight = c(130)
)
```

Step 11: Run k-NN (k = 3)

Next we apply the k-nearest neighbors (k-NN) algorithm using the knn() function from the class package. We set k = 3, meaning the algorithm will look at the 3 closest neighbors (based on height and weight) from the training data to decide which class the new data point most likely belongs to.

The knn() function compares the new data point (with height 66 and weight 130) to the training examples, identifies the 3 nearest neighbors, and assigns the most common label among them (either "Short" or "Tall") as the predicted class.

The result is printed and will show the predicted label—either "Short" or "Tall"—based on the majority vote of the 3 closest neighbors.

R Code
```
# Perform k-NN
predicted_label <- knn(train = train_data, test = test_data,
                       cl = train_labels, k = 3)


# View result
print(predicted_label)
```

Output
```
## [1] Short
## Levels: Short Tall
```

Wrap-Up

In this lab, you explored three key supervised learning algorithms used for classification: Decision Trees, Support Vector Machines (SVM), and k-Nearest Neighbors (k-NN). Each method uses labeled training data to learn how to predict outcomes for new, unseen cases. You saw how decision trees create rules based on input features, how SVM finds the optimal boundary between classes, and how k-NN relies on the majority vote from nearby examples.

Exercises

Supervised Learning (Classification)

This exercise set gives you hands-on practice with supervised classification techniques.

Dataset 1: Decision Tree – Student Pass Prediction

This dataset includes features about student behavior and whether they passed a course.

```
R Code
# Dataset 1: Student performance data
students <- data.frame(
  Attendance = c("High", "Low", "High", "Medium",
               "Medium", "Low","High", "Low",
               "High", "Medium"),
  Homework = c("Complete", "Incomplete", "Complete",
             "Complete", "Incomplete", "Incomplete",
             "Complete", "Incomplete", "Complete",
             "Complete"),
  Passed = c("Yes", "No", "Yes", "Yes", "No", "No", "
           Yes", "No", "Yes", "Yes")
)
```

1. Use the `rpart()` function to build a decision tree to predict `Passed` using `Attendance` and `Homework`. What is the resulting tree structure?
2. Visualize the decision tree using `rpart.plot()`. Paste the tree image.
3. According to the tree, which condition is most influential in predicting if a student passed?
4. Use your model to predict whether a student with `Attendance` =

"Low" and Homework = "Complete" would pass.

5. How would the tree change if the dataset were larger or had more predictors (like test scores)? Explain briefly.

Dataset 2: Support Vector Machine – Email Classification

This dataset represents emails classified by their word count and number of links.

```
R Code
# Dataset 2: Email data
emails <- data.frame(
  WordCount = c(50, 60, 300, 400, 70, 90, 280, 310),
  Links = c(0, 1, 5, 4, 1, 0, 6, 5),
  Category = as.factor(c("Personal", "Personal",
                         "Marketing", "Marketing",
                         "Personal", "Personal",
                         "Marketing", "Marketing"))
)
```

6. Train an SVM model to classify emails into "Personal" or "Marketing". Show your model code.

7. Plot the SVM decision boundary. Paste the resulting image.

8. Based on the plot, describe the separation between personal and marketing emails.

9. Predict the class for a new email with WordCount = 100 and Links = 2. What is the result?

10. What might happen if you added more ambiguous emails (e.g., marketing with low word count)? Would it affect the boundary?

Dataset 3: k-Nearest Neighbors – Fruit Size Classification

This dataset includes height and weight of fruit samples and their type (Apple or Orange).

```
R Code
# Dataset 3: Fruit measurements
fruit_train <- data.frame(
  height = c(5.1, 5.5, 5.7, 6.2, 6.5, 6.8),
  weight = c(120, 135, 145, 160, 170, 180)
)


fruit_labels <- c("Apple", "Apple", "Apple",
                  "Orange", "Orange", "Orange")


# New fruit to classify
fruit_test <- data.frame(height = 6.0, weight = 150)
```

11. Use `knn()` with `k = 3` to classify the new fruit. What class is it predicted to be?
12. Try again with `k = 5`. Does the prediction change? Why might that happen?
13. Based on the plot of training data (use `plot()`), where does the new fruit fall visually?

Lab 18

Sentiment Analysis

Sentiment analysis is a text mining technique used to determine whether a piece of text expresses a positive, negative, or neutral emotion. It is commonly applied to product reviews, social media posts, or any text where we want to understand public opinion or emotion.

In this lab, we'll use the tidytext package in R along with the bing sentiment lexicon to analyze the sentiment in a small set of sample product reviews. A sentiment lexicon is a collection of words that have been assigned predefined sentiment values such as positive, negative, or neutral. It is used in text analysis to estimate the overall sentiment of a document by matching words in the text to those in the lexicon.

Lesson Steps

Step 1: Load Required Libraries

First let's load and install required packages.

```
R Code
options(repos = c(CRAN = "https://cran.r-project.org"))
install.packages("tibble")
install.packages("tidytext")
install.packages("dplyr")


library(tibble)
library(tidytext)
library(dplyr)
```

Step 2: Create Sample Review Text

We' start with'll use a small set of three product reviews, each containing different emotional tones.

```
R Code
review_df <- tibble(text = c(
  "I love this product. It's amazing!",
  "This phone is terrible. The screen cracked.",
  "The device is okay, nothing special."
))
```

Step 3: Tokenize the Text

Tokenization breaks each sentence into individual words so we can analyze them.

```
R Code
review_words <- unnest_tokens(tbl = review_df,
                             output = word,
                             input = text)
```

Step 4: Load the Sentiment Lexicon

The bing lexicon (a reference table) categorizes words into either positive or negative sentiment.

```
R Code
sentiments <- get_sentiments("bing")
```

Step 5: Match Words with Sentiment Labels

This step joins the tokenized words with their associated sentiments using the Bing dictionary.

```
R Code
review_sentiment <- inner_join(review_words,
                               sentiments, by = "word")
```

In this step, we connect the words from our text with their matching sentiment labels using the Bing lexicon. For example, if the words "love," "the," "movie," and "boring" appear in the text, only "love" and "boring" will be matched because they exist in the Bing sentiment dictionary—"love" as positive and "boring" as negative. This process filters out words without sentiment and keeps only those that carry emotional meaning for analysis.

Step 6: Count Sentiment Words

Now we can see which words from the reviews matched with the sentiment dictionary and how often they occurred.

R Code
```
review_summary <- count(review_sentiment, word,
                        sentiment, sort = TRUE)
print(review_summary)
```

Output
```
## # A tibble: 4 x 3
##    word      sentiment     n
##    <chr>     <chr>     <int>
## 1 amazing   positive      1
## 2 cracked   negative      1
## 3 love      positive      1
## 4 terrible  negative      1
```

Step 7: Visualization

You can visualize the result using a bar chart:

R Code
```
options(repos = c(CRAN = "https://cran.r-project.org"))
install.packages("ggplot2")
library(ggplot2)
```

R Code

```
ggplot(review_summary, aes(x = reorder(word, n),
                   y = n, fill = sentiment)) +
  geom_col(show.legend = FALSE) +
  facet_wrap(~sentiment, scales = "free_y") +
  scale_fill_manual(values = c(
    "positive" = "#98C1D9",
    "negative" = "#EE6C4D"
  )) +
  labs(title = "Sentiment Word Counts",
       x = "Word", y = "Count") +
  coord_flip()
```

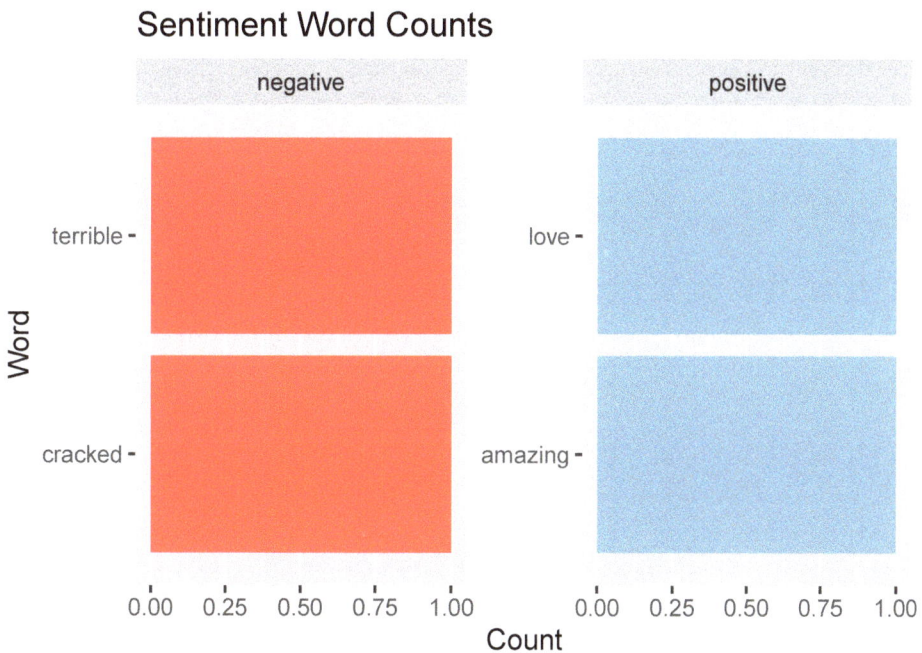

This bar chart shows the most common positive and negative words found in the text, based on matches from the Bing sentiment lexicon. Each bar represents a word that carries sentiment, and the length of the bar shows how many times that word appeared. The chart is split into two panels—one for positive words and one for negative words—so you can easily compare which words contribute most to the overall tone of the text.

Wrap-Up

In this lab, you learned how to perform basic sentiment analysis using the bing sentiment lexicon. The process began by breaking down text into individual words, a step known as tokenization. Next, these words were matched against a sentiment dictionary to identify whether they carried a positive or negative emotional tone. Finally, the matched words were counted and summarized to give an overall sense of the sentiment in the text. This simple yet powerful technique allows us to quickly analyze and summarize emotional tone in text data.

Exercises

Sentiment Analysis

These exercises will help you practice the core steps in sentiment analysis using `tidytext` and the `bing` lexicon in R. You'll tokenize text, join with sentiment labels, and summarize the results.

Dataset 1: Movie Reviews

The dataset below includes three brief movie review texts.

```
R Code
movie_reviews <- tibble(text = c(
  "The movie was fantastic and heartwarming.",
  "I hated every second of it. So boring!",
  "Some parts were good, but mostly forgettable."
))
```

1. Tokenize the movie reviews using `unnest_tokens()`. How many total words were extracted?
2. Join the tokenized words with the `bing` sentiment lexicon. How many words were matched with a sentiment?
3. Create a summary table showing how many positive and negative words appear. Which sentiment was more common?
4. Visualize the sentiment words using a bar chart as shown in the lab. Paste the chart or describe the key terms.
5. Identify one or two emotionally charged words that were not matched with a sentiment. Why might they be missing?

Dataset 2: Customer Service Tweets

This dataset simulates customer service feedback.

```
R Code
# Dataset 2: Simulated customer tweets
tweets <- tibble(text = c(
  "Absolutely terrible support. I waited an hour!",
  "Great service, fast and friendly staff.",
  "Not bad overall, but delivery was slow."
))
```

6. Tokenize the tweets and join with the Bing lexicon. How many sentiment words were found?

7. How does the tone differ between the first and second tweet based on the matched sentiment words?

8. Use count() to list all words matched and their sentiment. Which negative word is most frequent?

9. Create a sentiment bar chart. Paste the chart or summarize what it reveals.

10. If one tweet had no matched sentiment words, what might that indicate about the tone or vocabulary?

Dataset 3: Tech Product Reviews

This dataset includes three tech product reviews with mixed feedback.

R Code

```
# Dataset 3: Product reviews
tech_reviews <- tibble(text = c(
  "Excellent battery life but the camera is awful.",
  "Smooth performance, no issues, highly recommended!",
  "Crashes constantly and the interface is confusing."
))
```

11. After tokenizing and joining with Bing, how many positive and negative words are found across all reviews?

12. Create a side-by-side bar chart (faceted by sentiment) showing word counts. Paste or describe the result.

13. Which review contains both positive and negative words? What might this say about mixed sentiment?

14. One word in the review is "confusing." Was this matched in the sentiment lexicon? If not, how could you include such words in your analysis?

Lab 19

Basic Graphs and `ggplot2` in R

Visualizing data helps uncover patterns, trends, and outliers that might be hidden in tables of raw numbers. Whether you're exploring a dataset for the first time or presenting your findings to others, effective visuals can make your insights clearer and more impactful.

In this lab, you'll use ggplot2, a visualization package in R. Built on the Grammar of Graphics (hence gg), ggplot2 constructs plots by layering components, starting with the data and then adding elements such as points, bars, lines, and labels. This structured approach makes it easy to build and customize a wide variety of charts, even with minimal code.

This lab will focus on making three fundamental types of graphs that are widely used in data analysis. A bar chart helps compare values across categories. A line chart is ideal for showing changes over time. A scatter plot reveals relationships between two numeric variable.

Lesson Steps

Step 1: Install ggplot

Before you begin, make sure you have the package installed and loaded:

```
R Code
options(repos = c(CRAN = "https://cran.r-project.org"))
install.packages("ggplot2")  # Only run once
library(ggplot2)
```

Step 2: Bar Charts

Bar charts are one of the most common ways to present comparisons. They provide a simple and effective way to show differences in quantity, frequency, or count for distinct groups. Whether you're comparing product sales, survey responses, or population figures, bar charts make the differences visually clear.

Let's make a small dataset.

```
R Code
# Sample fruit sales data
fruit_data <- data.frame(
  Fruit = c("Apples", "Bananas", "Oranges", "Grapes"),
  Sales = c(120, 150, 90, 60)
)

# Create bar chart
ggplot(fruit_data, aes(x = Fruit, y = Sales)) +
  geom_bar(stat = "identity", fill = "#98C1D9") +
  labs(title = "Fruit Sales", x = "Fruit", y = "Units Sold")
```

Fruit Sales

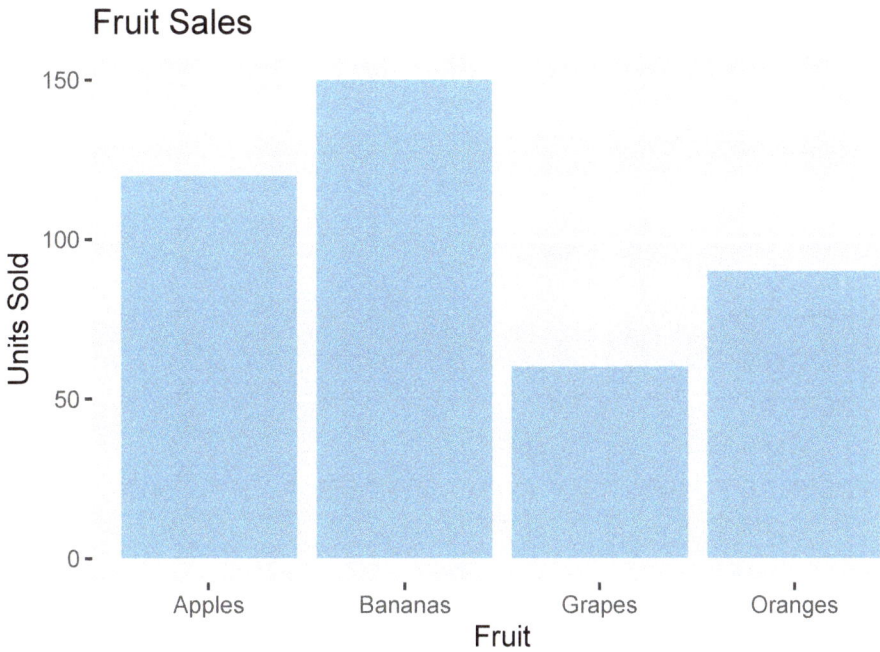

The result is an easy-to-read bar chart that shows bananas had the highest sales and grapes the lowest, making it immediately obvious which fruits performed best.

Step 3: Line Chart

Line charts are ideal for displaying trends over time. Line chart helps you see how values rise, fall, or stay consistent. This is especially useful for tracking progress, patterns, or seasonality.

Let's simulate some data.

R Code

```
# Weekly visitors data
visits <- data.frame(
  Week = paste("Week", 1:6),
  Visitors = c(300, 450, 500, 480, 520, 600)
)


# Create line chart
ggplot(visits, aes(x = Week, y = Visitors, group = 1)) +
  geom_line(color = "#293241", size = 1.2) +
  geom_point(color = "#293241") +
  labs(title = "Website Visitors Over Time", x = "Week",
       y = "Visitors")
```

Website Visitors Over Time

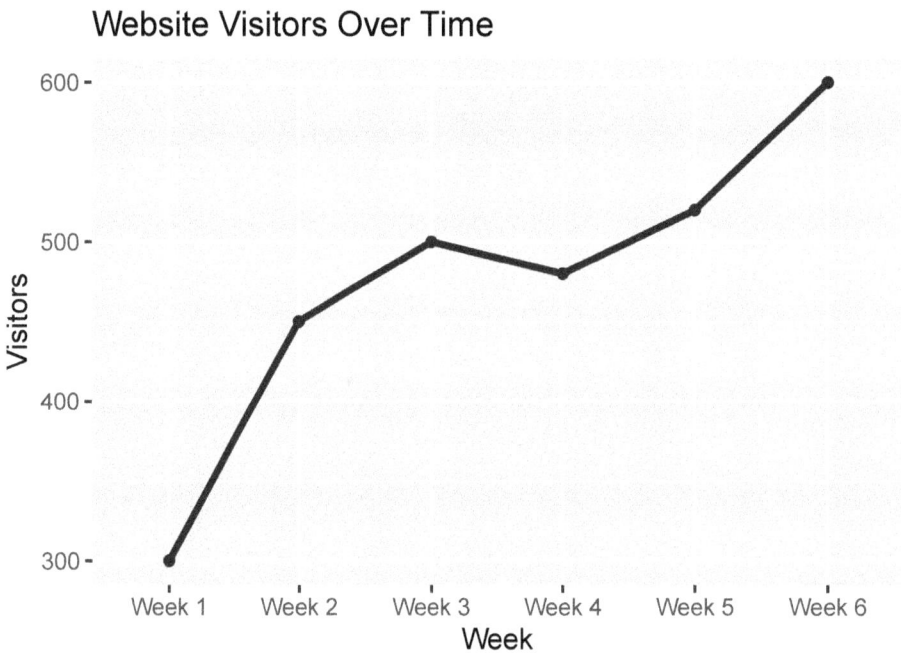

In this plot, a general upward trend in visitor numbers, with a slight dip in

Week 4 is revealed.

Step 4: Scatter Plot

Scatter plots are used to explore relationships between two continuous variables. They help us see if a connection exists—whether it's positive, negative, or none (actually measuring this is done with a metric known as a correlation covered in an earlier lab).

Let's simulate a data set with hours studied and test scores as our variables.

```
R Code
# Study data
study_data <- data.frame(
  Hours_Studied = c(1, 2, 3, 4, 5, 6, 7),
  Test_Score = c(55, 60, 65, 70, 75, 82, 88)
)


# Create scatter plot
ggplot(study_data, aes(x = Hours_Studied, y = Test_Score)) +
  geom_point(color = "#637D8D", size = 3) +
  labs(title = "Study Time vs. Test Score",
       x = "Hours Studied", y = "Test Score")
```

Study Time vs. Test Score

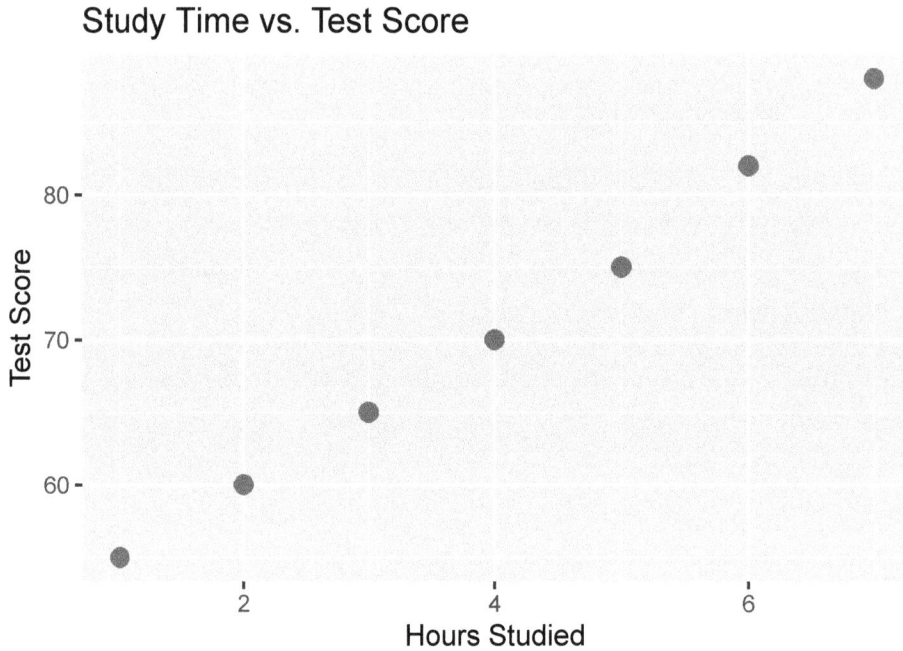

This scatter plot places each student's data point based on how many hours they studied (x-axis) and what score they earned on the test (y-axis). The result shows a clear positive relationship: as study time increases, so do test scores.

Wrap-Up

In this lab, you explored three essential types of data visualizations—bar charts, line charts, and scatter plots—using the ggplot2 package in R. Each graph type serves a different purpose: bar charts compare values across categories, line charts track changes over time, and scatter plots reveal relationships between continuous variables. Using meaningful visuals can enhance both data exploration and communication.

Exercises

Basic Graphs and `ggplot2`

In this exercise set, you will practice creating three common types of data visualizations using `ggplot2`: bar charts, line charts, and scatter plots. These plots help you explore and communicate patterns, relationships, and trends.

Dataset 1: Favorite Programming Languages (Bar Chart)

This dataset shows how many students in a class chose each programming language as their favorite.

```
R Code
# Dataset 1: Programming language preferences
language_data <- data.frame(
  Language = c("Python", "R", "JavaScript", "SQL", "C++"),
  Students = c(15, 12, 9, 8, 6)
)
```

1. Create a bar chart showing the number of students per programming language. Which language is most preferred?
2. Modify the bar chart to use a custom fill color (e.g., "#A8DADC"). Paste or describe the result.
3. What does `stat = "identity"` do in `geom_bar()`? Why is it needed here?
4. Adjust the bar chart to sort languages from most to least popular (hint: use `reorder()` in `aes()`).
5. Suppose another language "Rust" had 10 students. Add this to the dataset and replot. What changes?

Dataset 2: Monthly Book Sales (Line Chart)

This dataset tracks the number of books sold by a small publisher over six months.

```
R Code
# Dataset 2: Book sales over time
book_sales <- data.frame(
  Month = c("Jan", "Feb", "Mar", "Apr", "May", "Jun"),
  Units_Sold = c(200, 220, 210, 250, 270, 260)
)
```

6. Create a line chart showing book sales over time. Use points to mark each data value.
7. Add a descriptive title and axis labels to your chart. What overall trend do you observe?
8. Modify the line chart to use a different line color (e.g., "#FF6B6B"). What impact does this have visually?
9. Identify the month with the highest and lowest sales based on the chart.
10. How might this trend help the publisher make future decisions?

Dataset 3: Sleep and Productivity (Scatter Plot)

This dataset tracks hours of sleep and corresponding productivity scores for 8 people.

R Code

```
# Dataset 3: Sleep and productivity
sleep_data <- data.frame(
  Hours_Slept = c(4, 5, 6, 7, 7.5, 8, 8.5, 9),
  Productivity = c(50, 55, 60, 65, 70, 72, 74, 70)
)
```

11. Create a scatter plot showing the relationship between sleep hours and productivity.

12. Based on the plot, describe the pattern. Does more sleep always mean higher productivity?

13. Add a trend line to the scatter plot using `geom_smooth(method = "loess")`. What does it show?

14. Label the axes clearly and change the point color to dark green (`"#2A9D8F"`). Why might color be important in visual design?

15. Suggest one real-world use for a scatter plot like this in workplace or health analytics.

Lab 20

Best Practices for Graphs and Charts

Charts and graphs are powerful tools for communication. They can instantly clarify a pattern or insight that would take paragraphs to explain. But a poorly designed one can confuse, mislead, or even hide the story in your data. In this lab, you'll learn key best practices for creating clear, readable, and effective graphs in R using ggplot2.

Lesson Steps

Step 1: Only Show What Matters

Start by eliminating clutter. Extra layers, groupings, or colors might seem useful, but they often distract from the main message.

R Code

```
# Too much detail - stacked bar chart by gender
survey_data <- data.frame(
  Response = rep(c("Yes", "No", "Maybe"), each = 2),
  Gender = rep(c("Male", "Female"), 3),
  Count = c(30, 25, 20, 22, 10, 12)
)


ggplot(survey_data, aes(
  x = Response, y = Count,
  fill = Gender
)) +
  geom_bar(stat = "identity") +
  scale_fill_manual(values = c(
    "Male" = "#637D8D",
    "Female" = "#EE6C4D"
  )) +
  labs(
    title = "Detailed Survey Data",
    x = "Response", y = "Count"
  ) +
  theme_minimal()
```

Detailed Survey Data

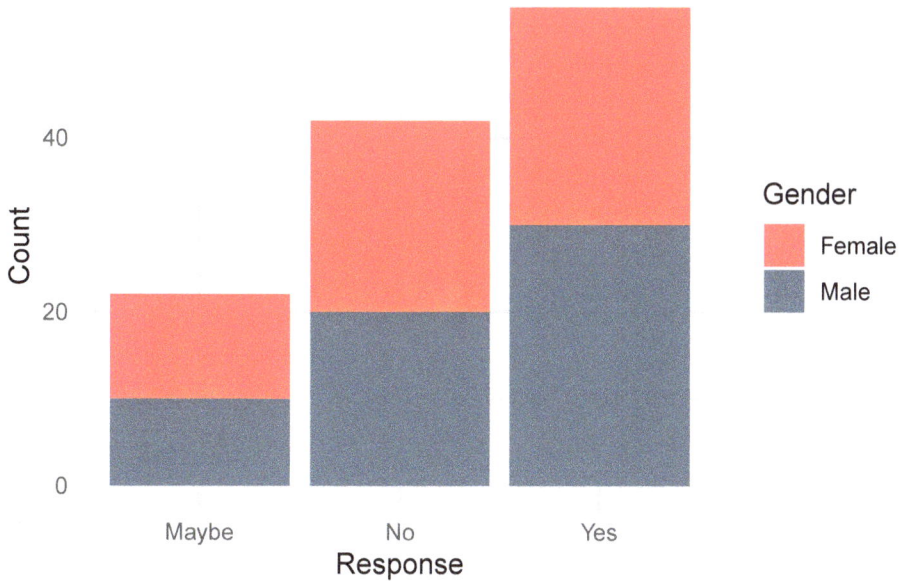

This chart stacks gender within each response, which adds visual complexity.

Now simplify it:

```
R Code
# Simplified - remove gender and show total
total_responses <- aggregate(Count ~ Response,
                             data = survey_data, sum)

ggplot(total_responses, aes(x = Response, y = Count)) +
  geom_bar(stat = "identity", fill = "#98C1D9") +
  labs(title = "Overall Survey Responses",
       x = "Response", y = "Count") +
  theme_minimal()
```

Overall Survey Responses

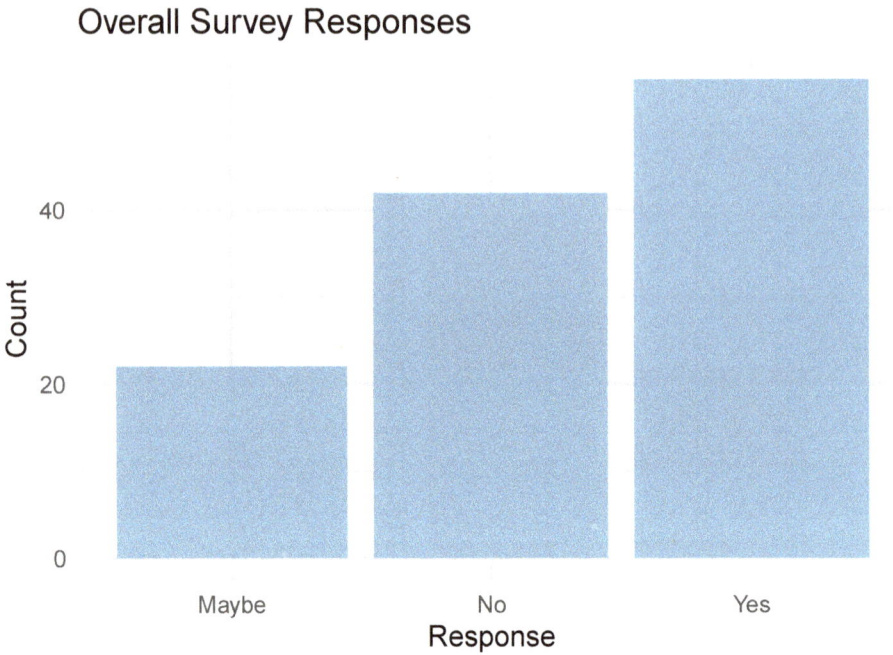

Focus on what supports your story. If details like subgroups aren't essential, leave them out.

Step 2: Use Clear, Readable Labels

Labels are not the place for shortcuts or technical abbreviations. Make them as readable as possible.

R Code
```
# Clear labels
fruit_data <- data.frame(
  Fruit = c("Apples", "Bananas", "Oranges"),
  Sales = c(120, 150, 100)
)


ggplot(fruit_data, aes(x = Fruit, y = Sales)) +
  geom_bar(stat = "identity", fill = "#3D5A80") +
  labs(title = "Fruit Sales in April", x = "Fruit Type",
       y = "Units Sold") +
  theme_minimal()
```

Fruit Sales in April

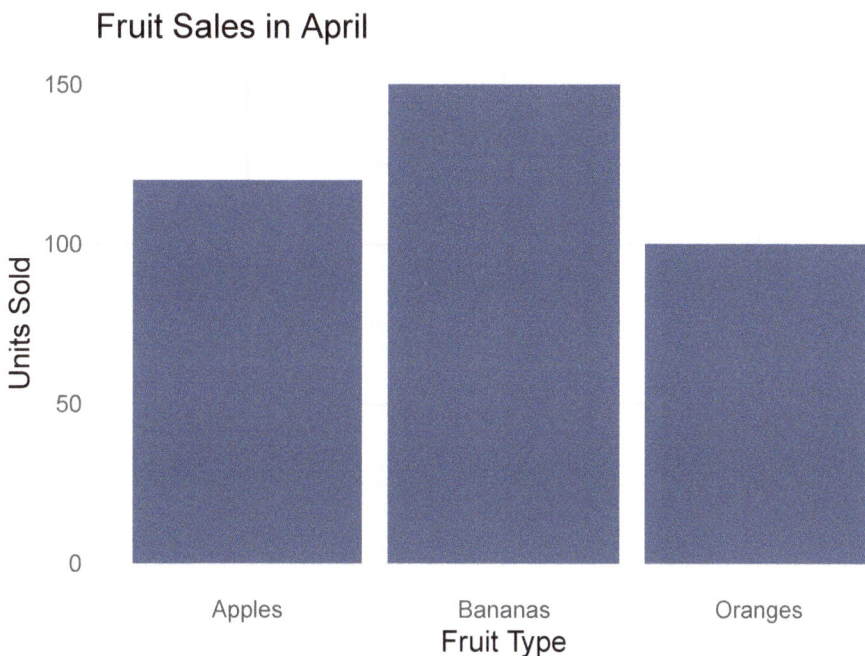

Compare this confusing version:

R Code
```
# Confusing labels
ggplot(fruit_data, aes(x = Fruit, y = Sales)) +
  geom_bar(stat = "identity", fill =  "#3D5A80") +
  labs(title = "frt_sl_apr", x = "frt", y = "cnt") +
  theme_minimal()
```

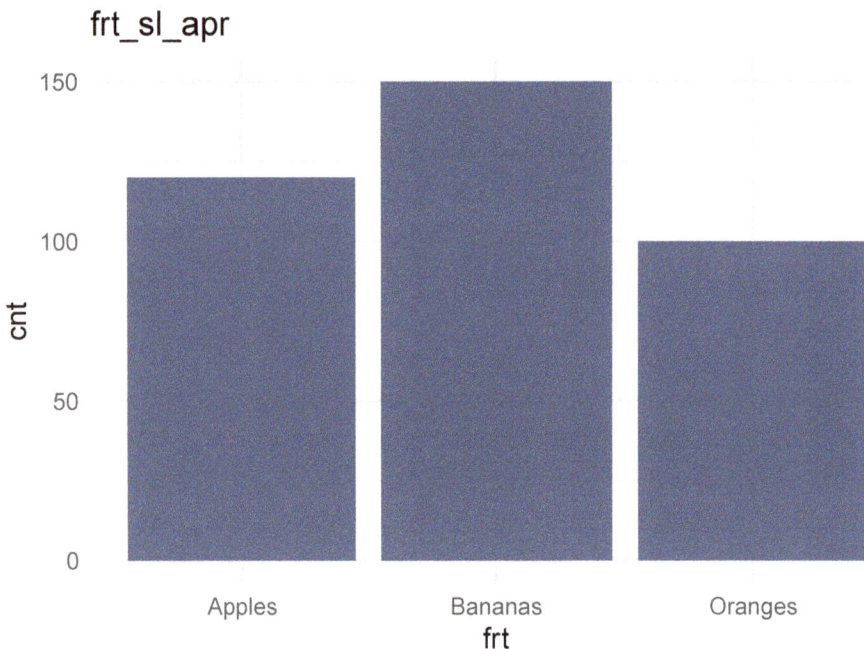

Always write titles and axis labels as if your audience is seeing the data for the first time.

Step 3. Choose Color Schemes Wisely

Colors should help the viewer—not confuse them. Avoid using red and green together or low-contrast combinations. Instead, use built-in palettes that are accessible and colorblind-friendly.

R Code

```
# Good color contrast using RColorBrewer
library(RColorBrewer)

ggplot(survey_data, aes(x = Response, y = Count,
                        fill = Gender)) +
  geom_bar(stat = "identity", position = "dodge") +
  scale_fill_brewer(palette = "Set2") +
  labs(title = "Responses by Gender", x = "Response",
       y = "Count") +
  theme_minimal()
```

Responses by Gender

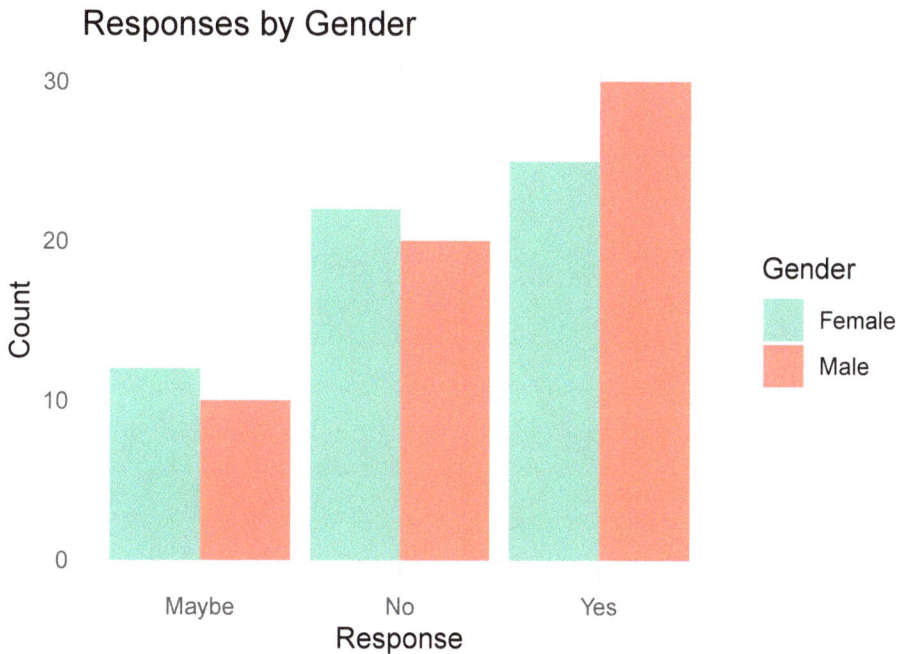

Now compare it with this poor example:

R Code

```
# Poor contrast (not colorblind-friendly)
ggplot(survey_data, aes(x = Response, y = Count,
                        fill = Gender)) +
  geom_bar(stat = "identity", position = "dodge") +
  scale_fill_manual(values = c("red", "green")) +
  labs(title = "Responses by Gender", x = "Response",
       y = "Count") +
  theme_minimal()
```

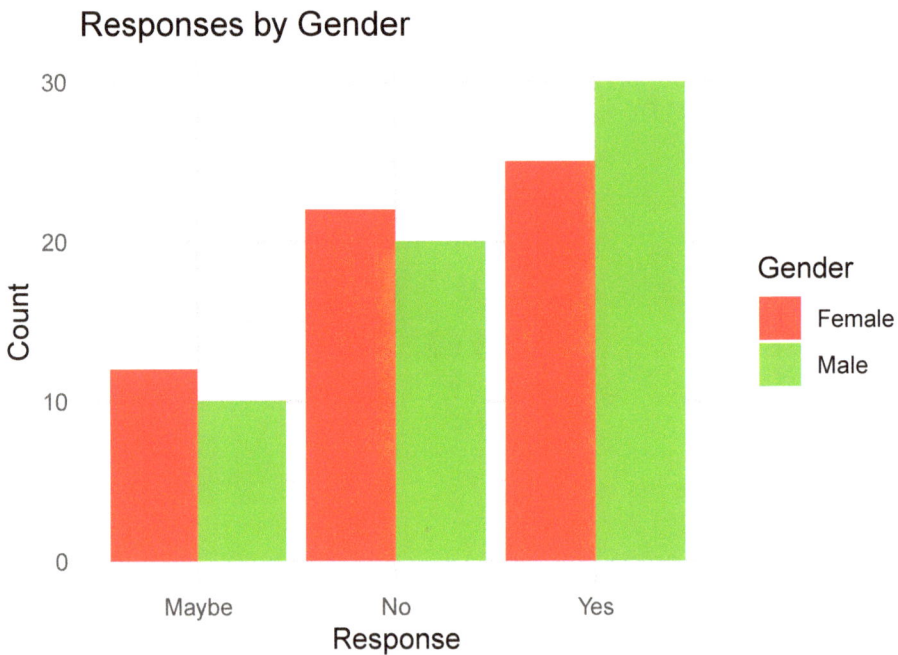

Responses by Gender

Use color to highlight and clarify, not decorate. Consider accessibility for all viewers.

Step 4: Avoid 3D Effects and Busy Designs

Simplicity helps your message shine. Fancy 3D effects or gradients can distract the viewer and make charts harder to interpret.

```
R Code
# Clean and simple chart design
ggplot(fruit_data, aes(x = Fruit, y = Sales)) +
  geom_bar(stat = "identity", fill = "#98C1D9") +
  labs(title = "Fruit Sales", x = "Fruit", y = "Sales") +
  theme_minimal()
```

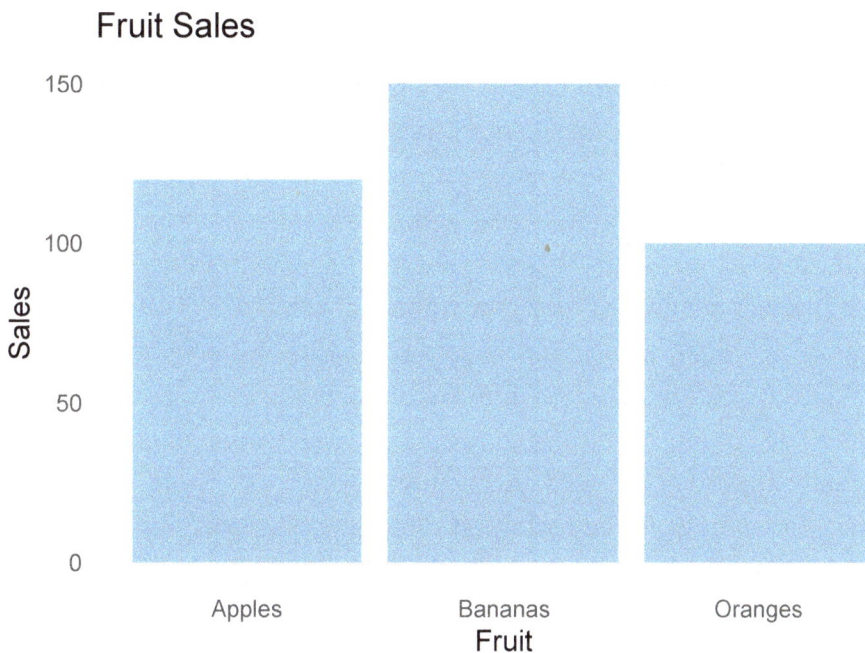

Fruit Sales

There's no clutter here, just clean design that directs attention to the data. Stick with flat, minimal design for maximum clarity.

Step 5: Keep It Focused

Every design choice in a graph—whether it's the axis scale, font, color, or label—should support the main message you're trying to communicate. Visual clutter or unnecessary decoration can distract from the story your data is telling. Aim for simplicity and clarity: shorten long titles, remove gridlines if they're not useful, and highlight the parts of the chart that matter most. As you design your visual, keep asking yourself: What's the key message? And does this element help communicate that? If the answer is no, it's probably best to remove or revise that element.

Wrap-Up

Effective data visualization is about making a visual that is clear and useful. Throughout this lab, you learned how seemingly small adjustments—such as refining labels, adjusting layout, selecting appropriate colors, and controlling the level of detail—can significantly enhance how well a chart communicates its message. The most successful visualizations focus solely on what matters, removing any distractions that could divert attention away from the core insight. Using plain-language labels helps ensure that the audience quickly understands the information being presented, while choosing accessible colors with strong contrast improves readability for everyone. It is equally important to avoid clutter, unnecessary 3D effects, and decorative elements that do not add informational value. Every aspect of the chart should serve the main message, reinforcing rather than confusing it.

Exercises

Best Practices for Graphs and Charts

In this exercise set, you'll apply core visualization principles that help make graphs clear, focused, and effective. You will revise charts, interpret design choices, and explain why certain styles work better than others.

Dataset 1: Streaming Platform Preferences

This dataset shows how many people in a survey prefer each streaming platform.

```
R Code
streaming_data <- data.frame(
  Platform = c("Netflix", "Hulu", "Disney+", "HBO Max"),
  Count = c(50, 20, 30, 25)
)
```

1. Create a bar chart showing platform preferences using `ggplot2`. Keep the design minimal.
2. Now modify the chart to use poor design: change the fill color of each bar to something different and add a distracting title like `"plt_prf_dist"`. What makes it harder to read?
3. Fix your chart from question 2 by writing a clear title and axis labels. Explain why your revision is better.
4. Suppose you're only interested in the most popular platform. Redraw the chart to focus just on Netflix.
5. Why is removing clutter important in a bar chart? Give one example from your plot.

Dataset 2: Pet Adoption by Type and Gender

This dataset shows pet adoptions by pet type and adopter gender.

```
R Code
adoption_data <- data.frame(
  Pet = rep(c("Dog", "Cat", "Rabbit"), each = 2),
  Gender = rep(c("Male", "Female"), 3),
  Count = c(35, 40, 30, 25, 10, 15)
)
```

6. Create a grouped bar chart showing adoption counts by pet and gender. Use `position = "dodge"`.
7. First, use `scale_fill_manual(values = c("red", "green"))`. What problem might some viewers have?
8. Now fix the chart by using a colorblind-friendly palette (e.g., `scale_fill_brewer(palette = "Set2")`). Why is this better?
9. Add a clear title and axis labels. Why does label clarity matter for understanding?
10. Remove the legend and label each bar directly with its count. When might this be useful?

Dataset 3: Daily Coffee Sales

This dataset shows sales of coffee units across 5 weekdays.

```
R Code
coffee_data <- data.frame(
  Day = c("Mon", "Tue", "Wed", "Thu", "Fri"),
  Sales = c(100, 110, 105, 130, 125)
)
```

11. Make a simple bar chart of coffee sales by day.
12. Add a 3D effect (e.g., simulate shading or gradient if possible). Why might this be harmful to clarity?
13. Remove all extra effects. Use `theme_minimal()` and a flat color (e.g., "#A8DADC"). Describe the difference.
14. Shrink the y-axis to start at 100 instead of 0. What message does that send? Is it misleading?
15. Based on everything you've practiced, list three principles for effective chart design in your own words.

Lab 21

Visualizing Geographic Data

Maps are among the most intuitive and impactful tools for visualizing data that has a geographic dimension. Whether you're studying population density, tracking store locations, or examining public health trends, maps provide a way to instantly reveal spatial patterns and anomalies that might be difficult to detect in traditional tables or static charts. By placing data directly on a geographic canvas, maps help connect numbers to real-world places, making insights more relatable and actionable.

In this lab, you will learn how to work effectively with geographic data using R's sf package. You will create several types of maps with ggplot2, including choropleth maps that use color shading to represent values by region, dot maps that pinpoint locations, and heat maps that highlight areas of concentration.

Lesson Steps

Step 1: Load Required Packages

Install the packages if you haven't already. These are needed to handle spatial data and visualizations.

```
R Code
options(repos = c(CRAN = "https://cran.r-project.org"))
# Install if needed
install.packages("ggplot2")
install.packages("sf")
install.packages("dplyr")


library(ggplot2)
library(sf)
library(dplyr)
```

Step 2: Load and Plot a Basic Map

We'll start with a built-in shapefile of North Carolina counties included in the sf package. This file shows the geographic boundaries of counties.

```
R Code
# Load NC county shapefile (from sf package)
usa <- st_read(system.file("shape/nc.shp", package = "sf"),
               quiet = TRUE)


# Plot basic map
ggplot(data = usa) +
  geom_sf(fill = "#98C1D9") +
  labs(title = "North Carolina County Map")
```

North Carolina County Map

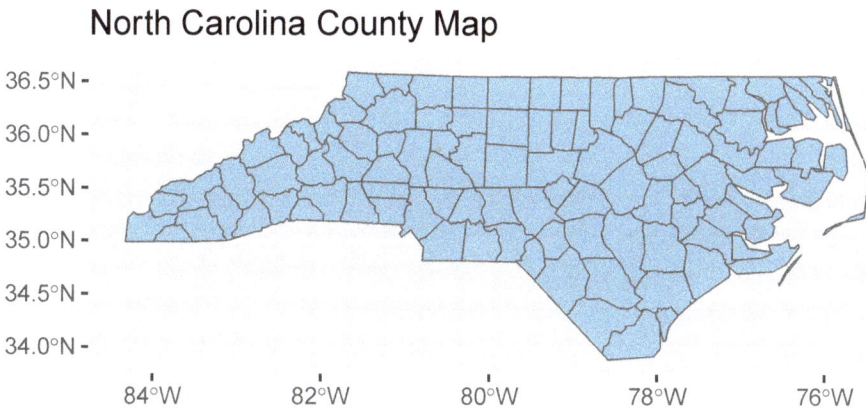

This creates a simple area map with clear geographic outlines.

Step 3: Choropleth Map

Choropleth maps use color to show values (like population or cases) for each region.

R Code

```
# Simulate fake population density data
set.seed(123)
usa$pop_density <- runif(nrow(usa), min = 50, max = 500)


# Plot choropleth
ggplot(usa) +
  geom_sf(aes(fill = pop_density)) +
  scale_fill_viridis_c() +
  labs(title = "Fake Population Density by County",
       fill = "Pop. Density")
```

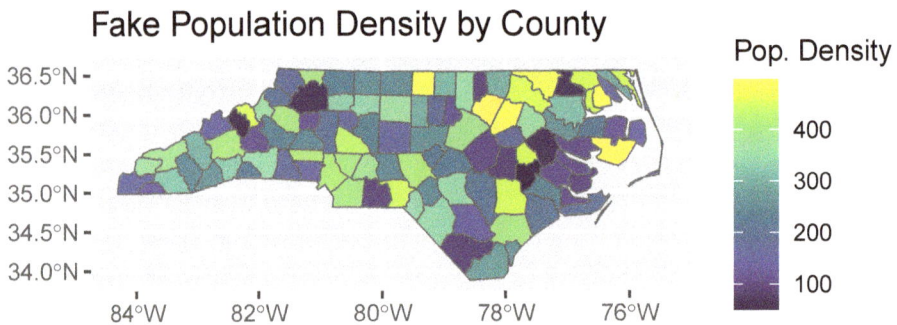

Fake Population Density by County

Here, each county is shaded based on a simulated density value.

Step 4: Dot Map

Dot maps show specific locations, such as stores or events.

```
R Code
# Simulate store locations
stores <- data.frame(
  lon = c(-78.6, -78.5, -78.7),
  lat = c(35.8, 35.9, 35.75)
)

ggplot() +
  geom_sf(data = usa, fill = "gray95") +
  geom_point(data = stores, aes(x = lon, y = lat),
             color = "#3D5A80", size = 3) +
  labs(title = "Store Locations (Point Data)")
```

Store Locations (Point Data)

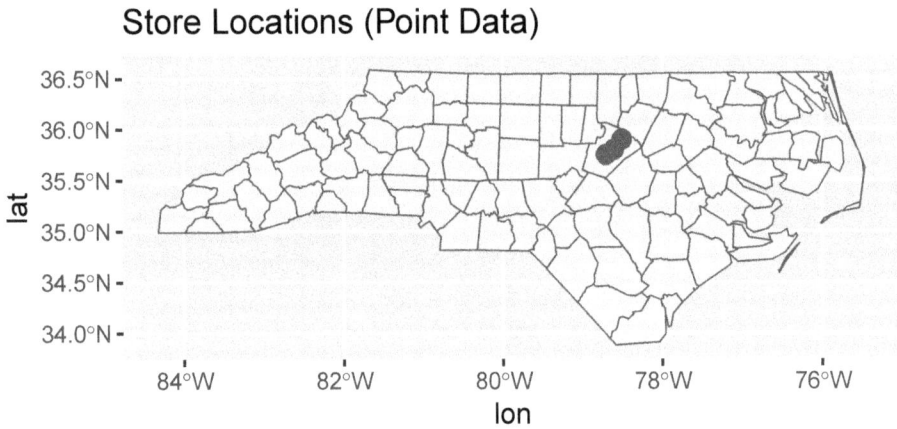

Each dot marks a location on the map.

Step 5: Heat Map

Heat maps show the intensity of points in a region. They're great for things like traffic or crime data.

Areas with more overlapping points appear darker and more intense.

Step 6: Case Study – Public Health

Maps are often used to track disease outbreaks or other public health data.

R Code

```
# Simulate reported disease cases by county
set.seed(456)
usa$cases <- sample(20:200, nrow(usa), replace = TRUE)

ggplot(usa) +
  geom_sf(aes(fill = cases)) +
  scale_fill_gradient(low = "#FFF6E5", high = "#3D5A80") +
  labs(title = "Reported Disease Cases by County",
       fill = "Cases")
```

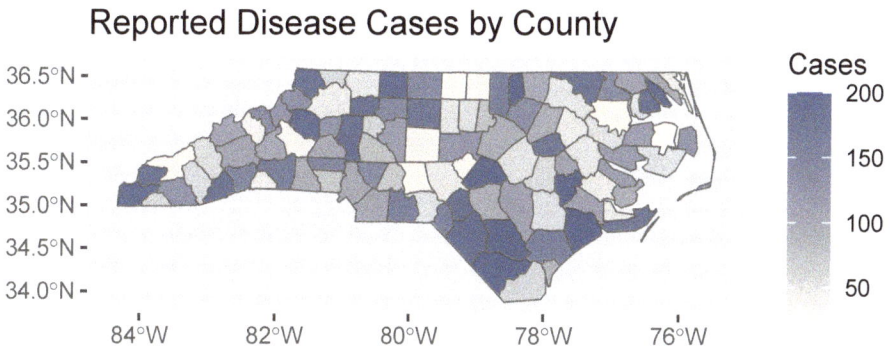

Reported Disease Cases by County

This map highlights regional differences in disease burden.

Wrap-Up

In this lab, you explored ways to visualize geographic data. You began by plotting spatial boundaries using the sf package and the geom_sf() function, which allow for straightforward handling and visualization of spatial data in R. From there, you developed choropleth maps that effectively represent values by area through color shading, providing a clear view of regional differences. You also practiced making dot maps to pinpoint specific locations and heat maps to reveal patterns of density across space. You also saw that different map types serve different communicative purposes, whether highlighting regional variation, exact locations, or intensity of phenomena.

Exercises

Visualizing Geographic Data

In this exercise set, you will work with geographic datasets using R's `sf` package and `ggplot2`. You'll create and interpret different types of maps: a choropleth showing unemployment rates by state and a dot map showing airport locations across the US.

Dataset 1: US States with Simulated Unemployment Rates

```
R Code
options(repos = c(CRAN = "https://cran.r-project.org"))
install.packages("maps")


# NOTE if necessary also install packages
library(sf)
library(ggplot2)
library(dplyr)
library(maps)
```

R Code

```
# Load US states shapefile
states_sf <- st_as_sf(map("state",
  plot = FALSE,
  fill = TRUE
))


# Simulate unemployment rates (percentage) by state
set.seed(123)
states_sf$unemployment <- runif(nrow(states_sf),
  min = 2.5, max = 10
)
```

1. Use `summary(states_sf$unemployment)` to find the minimum and maximum unemployment rates. What are they?

2. Create a choropleth map of the US states colored by unemployment rate using `geom_sf()`. Include a color legend labeled "Unemployment Rate (%)". What states appear to have the highest unemployment visually?

3. Print the class of the object `states_sf`. What type of object is it?

4. Which R package provides the `st_as_sf()` function? What does it do?

5. How many states are represented in this dataset? Use `nrow(states_sf)` to find out.

Dataset 2: US Airports Locations

```
R Code
# Create a data frame of sample US airport coordinates
airports <- data.frame(
  airport = c(
    "Los Angeles Intl", "Chicago O'Hare",
    "Atlanta Hartsfield", "Denver Intl",
    "Miami Intl"
  ),
  lon = c(
    -118.4085, -87.9048, -84.4277, -104.6737,
    -80.2906
  ),
  lat = c(33.9416, 41.9742, 33.6407, 39.8561, 25.7959)
)

# Convert to sf object with geographic coordinates
airports_sf <- st_as_sf(airports,
  coords = c(
    "lon",
    "lat"
  ),
  crs = 4326
)
```

6. What is the class of the `airports_sf` object? Use `class()` to check.

7. Plot the US states map (from Dataset 1) with airport locations as points overlaid using `geom_sf()`. What function do you use to add points?

8. Change the point color of airports to red and increase their size to 4 in

the plot. Paste the updated ggplot code.

9. Using `st_coordinates(airports_sf)`, extract the longitude and latitude coordinates. What are the coordinates for "Denver Intl"?

10. How many airports are included in this dataset? Use `nrow()` to find out.

Lab 22

Storytelling with Data

Data storytelling goes beyond simply presenting numbers—it is about communicating insights in a way that truly connects with an audience. When done effectively, storytelling with data provides context, highlights key changes, and helps people remember and act on the information they receive. Rather than overwhelming viewers with raw figures, good data storytelling guides them through a meaningful sequence that explains what happened, when it happened, and why it matters.

In this lab, you will create a basic line plot that tracks website traffic over time. You will learn how to highlight important events, such as the launch of a marketing campaign, using annotations and color to draw attention to key insights.

Lesson Steps

Step 1: Setup

Start by loading the necessary library and creating simulated data that represents weekly website visits over a 10-week period.

R Code
```
options(repos = c(CRAN = "https://cran.r-project.org"))
install.packages('ggplot2')
# Load required package
library(ggplot2)
```

R Code
```
# Create simulated weekly website traffic data
traffic_data <- data.frame(
  Week = 1:10,
  Visits = c(500, 520, 480, 470, 600, 1200, 1100,
             900, 700, 650)
)
```

This data set reflects a typical pattern of stable traffic, a marketing campaign launch (Week 5), a traffic peak (Week 6), and a gradual decline afterward.

Step 2: Create a Basic Line Plot

This step builds a simple line chart showing traffic over time.

R Code
```
ggplot(traffic_data, aes(x = Week, y = Visits)) +
  geom_line(color = "#637D8D", size = 1) +
  geom_point(size = 3, color = "#637D8D") +
  labs(title = "Weekly Website Visits Over Time",
       x = "Week",
       y = "Number of Visits") +
  theme_minimal()
```

Weekly Website Visits Over Time

This chart gives a clean view of how visits changed each week but doesn't yet tell a story.

Step 3: Add Highlights and Annotations to Tell the Story

Now, you'll turn this basic chart into a visual narrative by highlighting key events and adding explanatory text.

R Code

```
ggplot(traffic_data, aes(x = Week, y = Visits)) +
  geom_line(color = "#637D8D", size = 1) +
  geom_point(size = 3, color = "#637D8D") +


  # Highlight campaign launch (Week 5)
  geom_point(data = traffic_data[traffic_data$Week == 5, ],
             aes(x = Week, y = Visits),
             color = "#EE6C4D", size = 5) +


  # Highlight traffic peak (Week 6)
  geom_point(data = traffic_data[traffic_data$Week == 6, ],
             aes(x = Week, y = Visits),
             color = "#293241", size = 5) +


  # Add annotations
  annotate("text", x = 5, y = 620, label = "Campaign Launch",
           color = "#EE6C4D", hjust = 0) +
  annotate("text", x = 6, y = 1250,
           label = "Traffic Peak High user engagement",
           color = "#293241", hjust = 0) +
  labs(title = "Website Traffic During Marketing Campaign",
       subtitle = "Campaign launch caused spike",
       x = "Week",
       y = "Number of Visits") +
  theme_minimal()
```

Website Traffic During Marketing Campaign
Campaign launch caused spike

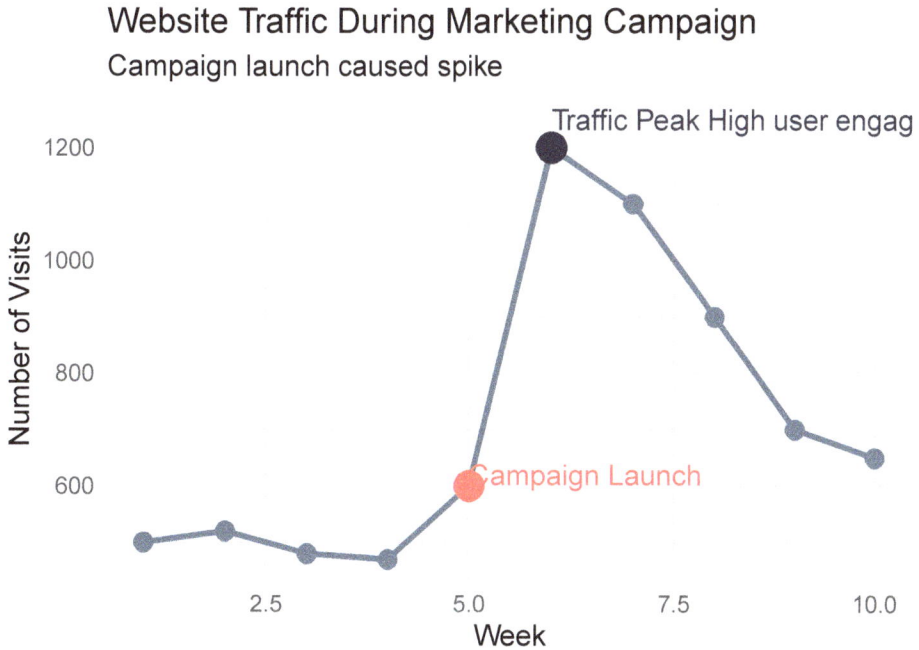

This annotated chart guides the viewer: from the flat baseline, to the campaign launch, to the dramatic peak in Week 6, and the gradual return to a new normal.

Wrap-Up

This lab demonstrated how to move beyond simply plotting data to telling a clear and meaningful story. The key takeaways emphasize that good data stories reveal not only what changed but why it matters. Thoughtful visual design strengthens the message, making it easier for audiences to understand and remember. This storytelling approach is essential in real-world contexts such as dashboards, business presentations, and public reports, where clarity and persuasion are crucial.

Exercises

Storytelling with Data

This exercise helps you practice creating line plots that highlight important events, use annotations for explanations, and tell a compelling data-driven story.

Dataset 1: Website Visits with a Marketing Campaign

Create this dataset in R:

```
R Code
# Dataset 1: Weekly website visits with a
# marketing campaign launch at Week 4
website_visits <- data.frame(
  Week = 1:10,
  Visits = c(400, 420, 410, 700, 1200, 1150, 950,
             800, 750, 700)
)
```

1. Plot a basic line chart showing Visits over Week using ggplot2.

2. Identify the week with the highest visits and write the week number.

3. Modify your plot to highlight the marketing campaign launch at Week 4 using a distinct color and larger point.

4. Add an annotation on the plot labeling Week 4 as "Campaign Launch." Which function did you use?

5. Describe briefly how the campaign affected website visits based on the plot.

Dataset 2: Daily Sales with a Promotion Event

Create this dataset in R:

```
R Code
# Dataset 2: Daily sales over 14 days with
# a promotion starting on Day 6
daily_sales <- data.frame(
  Day = 1:14,
  Sales = c(50, 55, 53, 52, 60, 130, 140, 135,
            120, 115, 110, 105, 100, 95)
)
```

6. Create a line plot of Sales over Day with points marked for each day.

7. Highlight the promotion start day (Day 6) with a different color and size point on your plot.

8. Add a text annotation near Day 6 that says "Promotion Start" in blue color.

9. On which day was the peak sales recorded? Provide the day and sales number.

10. Write 2–3 sentences explaining the impact of the promotion on daily sales.

www.ingramcontent.com/pod-product-compliance
Lightning Source LLC
Chambersburg PA
CBHW051722210326
41597CB00032B/5571